PUFFIN BOOKS

THE ARTHASHASTRA FOR CHILDREN

Deepa Agarwal is an author, poet and translator with over sixty published books for children and adults. She is a regular contributor to magazines and journals in India and abroad and has curated numerous anthologies. Her writing focuses on themes of gender equality, social justice and environmental preservation.

Deepa Agarwal has received several accolades and awards, including the NCERT National Award for Children's Literature for her picture book *Ashok's New Friends* and recognition on the IBBY Honour List for her historical fiction *Caravan to Tibet*. Her non-fiction work, *Journey to the Forbidden City*, was honoured on the Parag Honour List 2020 and was a finalist for the Neev Book Award 2021.

ADVANCE PRAISE FOR THE BOOK

'As Deepa Agarwal remarks, there is no book for children on Kautilya's Arthashastra. The reason is simple. It is not an easy one to write, and it takes a skilled author like Deepa Agarwal to write or even think of such a book. A relatively dry subject comes wonderfully alive, aided by some beautiful illustrations and a comprehensive introduction' —Bibek Debroy, economist

'This book does a marvellous job of presenting the essence of Kautilya's Arthashastra in a very interesting form. Proving, through modern parallels, that most of our laws can be traced back to Kautilya's ideas, Deepa Agarwal knits the past and present into one fluid, engrossing tale'—Devika Rangachari, author and historian

ALSO IN PUFFIN BY DEEPA AGARWAL

Caravan to Tibet
Puffin Lives: Rani Laxmibai
Puffin Lives: Chanakya
Journey to the Forbidden City
Chandrakanta
Listen, O King!

THE
ARTHASHASTRA
FOR CHILDREN

DEEPA AGARWAL

Illustrations by Radhika Dinesh

PUFFIN BOOKS

An imprint of Penguin Random House

PUFFIN BOOKS

USA | Canada | UK | Ireland | Australia
New Zealand | India | South Africa | China | Singapore

Puffin Books is part of the Penguin Random House group of companies
whose addresses can be found at global.penguinrandomhouse.com

Published by Penguin Random House India Pvt. Ltd
4th Floor, Capital Tower 1, MG Road,
Gurugram 122 002, Haryana, India

Penguin
Random House
India

First published in Puffin Books by Penguin Random House India 2023

Text copyright © Deepa Agarwal 2023
Illustrations copyright © Radhika Dinesh 2023

10 9 8 7 6 5 4 3 2

ISBN 9780143455318

Typeset in Adobe Garamond Pro by Manipal Technologies Limited, Manipal

Printed at Repro India Limited

www.penguin.co.in

Scan QR code to access the
Penguin Random House India website

MIX
Paper from
responsible sources
FSC® C047271

This is a legitimate digitally printed version of the book and therefore might not
have certain extra finishing on the cover.

To my beloved parents who taught me that the pursuit of knowledge is endless . . .

TABLE OF CONTENTS

Author's Note   ix

Introduction: What is the Arthashastra?   xiii

1. All About Kingship   1
2. What Is a Well-Organized State?   25
3. How to Make a Country Prosperous   48
4. How Were Funds to be Raised?   67
5. Babudom According to Kautilya   79
6. Towards Justice and an Orderly Society   92
7. About Spies and Secret Agents   108
8. Foreign Policy—Allies and Enemies,
    War and Peace   118
9. The Business of Making War   154

Selected Bibliography   175
Acknowledgments   179

AUTHOR'S NOTE

Many years ago, I had a chance to write a biography of Chanakya in the Puffin Lives series. Writing biographies is something I enjoy, as the research process brings you close to the person being studied, and the lives of historical figures are always inspiring. I had the opportunity to read Kautilya's (also known as Chanakya) famous work, the Arthashastra. Dr L.N. Rangarajan's translation was the one I found most accessible, and I delved into it to gain a better understanding of the man behind it. The experience was truly enlightening. The scale of the work, the depth of its ideas, and its timeless teachings left me in awe. It was remarkable to learn that such a monumental work was produced in our country centuries ago, and even the story of its rediscovery was captivating.

It made me realize that while we know about Kautilya and his credited treatise on statecraft, the Arthashastra, not many of us are familiar with the extensive list of topics it covers. From kingly duties and state administration to justice systems, law enforcement, urban planning, foreign relations, defence, and even consumer rights—Chanakya covered it all. It seemed as if no aspect of governance had escaped his attention. In fact, he addressed issues that policymakers in modern times haven't fully explored. What's more astonishing is that over two thousand years later, many of his theories remain relevant and continue to be applied in various fields.

I found myself wondering why I hadn't discovered the Arthashastra earlier. It felt like stumbling upon a crucial part of our heritage by chance. Of course, it's not a text for light reading. Our children are well-acquainted with epics like Ramayana and Mahabharata, as well as tales from the Panchatantra and Jatakas. Then why shouldn't they also be introduced to this great treatise? This thought persisted in my mind: what if someone created an abridged version of this tome, retold in a child-friendly style while preserving its essence and sparking young readers' interest in the seemingly dry subject of statecraft?

Now, a decade has passed since *Chanakya, the Master of Statecraft*, was published. The idea of a version of the Arthashastra tailored for young readers had lingered in my mind all this time. I often dismissed it as an impractical notion, yet it resurfaced persistently. Finally, during the pandemic, I shared the idea with my wonderful publisher at Puffin, Sohini Mitra, with whom I've collaborated on many other projects. I hesitated because I wasn't entirely sure myself, but she embraced the idea and that's how the journey began.

To be honest, this has been one of the most challenging books I've worked on. It wasn't until I sat down to work on it that I realized the difficulty of the task. Moreover, the pandemic further slowed my progress. Eventually, I completed the first draft, but it was quite unwieldy. Thankfully, with the assistance of my exceptional editors at Puffin and their insightful suggestions, the manuscript began to take shape, and I actually started enjoying the revision process. It felt like a battle with an angel—intense but incredibly enriching.

I've mentioned this before, and I reiterate it now—the Arthashastra is a priceless gem from our country's past. What you have here is a significantly modified version, yet my hope is that it will give children a glimpse of this remarkable work. Perhaps some of them will be curious enough to delve deeper into it at a later stage.

Deepa Agarwal,
August 2023

INTRODUCTION

WHAT IS THE ARTHASHASTRA?

AN AMAZING DISCOVERY

The year was 1904. In Mysore, Rudrapatna Shamasastry was examining ancient palm leaf manuscripts at the Mysore Oriental Library. The library possessed thousands of these precious, though extremely fragile, texts. As a librarian, it was his job to sift through the numerous manuscripts the library had acquired and classify them. This was not a task that any ordinary librarian could perform. Only a scholar with immaculate knowledge of Sanskrit and various ancient scripts was capable of handling such a duty efficiently and Shamasastry possessed this expertise.

Shamasastry began his education in his hometown, Rudrapatna, a village on the banks of the Kaveri River. A brilliant student, he continued his Sanskrit studies in Mysore and graduated from Madras University. Not only did he master classical Sanskrit but also learned Prakrit, Kannada, English, German and French.

No wonder Sir Sheshadri Iyer, the dewan or chief minister of the then princely state of Mysore, considered him the right candidate for the librarian's role at the Mysore Government Oriental Library in Mysore and recommended him highly.

It was a demanding task to assess these texts—rare relics of India's ancient literary traditions. But Shamasastry found his work exciting and rewarding. For him, each manuscript was like a precious heritage, and he felt privileged to have the opportunity to handle these sometimes almost forgotten writings.

When the library was set up under the patronage of Krishna Raja Wadiyar IV, the Maharaja of Mysore, many people who possessed such manuscripts came forward to deposit them at the library. Most of these had been preserved over generations in families with a tradition of learning. A few days ago, a pandit from Tanjore had appeared with a large pile of palm leaf manuscripts, and the librarian was reading them with his usual interest and curiosity. One glance informed him that they were written in the Grantha script, which had been commonly used to write Sanskrit in the Tamil-speaking areas of South India since the fifth century CE. The word *grantha* means 'knot' in Sanskrit and was used for written manuscripts since the palm leaf strips were tied together with a knot.

Intrigued, Shamasastry bent to peer closely at the writing on the delicate old document.

As he looked at a particular leaf, something made him pause. Carefully, he proceeded to the following one, and a peculiar sensation crept over his skin. His eyes began to speed over the writing, and his hands itched to riffle through the rest of the manuscript. With some effort, he controlled himself and reread the leaf thoroughly. A faint smile lit his face as he continued, breathless with anticipation. 'Is it possible?' was the thought that sprang into his head as he read on with mounting excitement.

When he had finished reading the manuscript, Shamasastry took a deep breath and folded his hands, sending up a prayer of thanks. His gut feeling was right; this was a discovery beyond belief—one of the greatest treasures of ancient India. The palm leaf manuscript he held in his hand was the long lost Arthashastra of Kautilya!

He rushed to inform his superiors about his find. The moment they heard, they hurried to look at the manuscript, overwhelmed by the news.

The Arthashastra was known to be the seminal treatise on the art of government, compiled by Kautilya, the prime minister of Chandragupta Maurya, who established the first great Indian empire. References to it had been found in the works of ancient writers like Dandin, Bana, Vishnusarma, Mallinathasuri and Megasthenes, the Greek historian, among others. However, to date, not a single copy had been located. It was believed that all copies of this great work had been lost to posterity.

This made it a finding momentous beyond belief. It would establish the fact that Indians had developed a sophisticated system of administration and demolish the theory that they acquired knowledge of statecraft from the Greeks—an opinion held by many scholars from the West.

It took Shamasastry a long time to go through the whole pile of palm leaves. However, a celebratory emotion was already mounting in the corridors of the library. In no time, the news spread like wildfire not only in the country but also throughout the world. Shamasastry's discovery was hailed with great joy and enthusiasm by scholars of ancient Indian history. One can well imagine that scores of historians itched to get a glimpse of this precious work.

Soon after, Shamasastry began the enormous task of transcribing and editing his find, and when the Sanskrit version was published in 1909, it became accessible to the public. Subsequently, he translated the text into English, which brought it to a wider audience. Between 1905 and 1909, Shamasastry published English translations of the text in installments in the journals *Indian Antiquary* and *Mysore Review*. In the course of time, the text was translated into German and French as well.

This great contribution brought lasting fame to Shamasastry, who received numerous honours. The Oriental University in Washington DC awarded him a doctorate in 1919 and Calcutta University followed suit in 1921. He was inducted as a Fellow of the Royal Asiatic Society. He also received the prestigious Campbell Memorial gold medal.

Apart from these honours, the Maharaja of Mysore granted him the title of Arthashastra Visharada, the Government of India bestowed that of Mahamahopadhyaya and Vidyalankara and the Varanasi Sanskrit Mandali that of Panditaraja.

Shamasastry's fame spread so far and wide that when the Maharaja of Mysore visited Germany for a conference, the vice-chancellor of a German University asked him if he was from the 'Mysore of Shamasastry'. When he returned home, the Maharaja told the scholar, 'In Mysore, we are the Maharaja and you are our subject, but in Germany, you are the master and people recognize us by your name and fame.'

The Arthashastra mentions the Rajarshi as the ideal king. Interestingly, Maharaja Krishna Raja Wadiyar IV was referred to as Rajarshi by Mahatma Gandhi and universally praised for his efficient administration and benevolence. He is referred to as the Father of Modern Mysore.

WHY IS THE ARTHASHASTRA SO IMPORTANT?

We can describe the discovery of the Arthashastra as a fortunate accident, happening as it did in 1905. The first Sanskrit edition, published in 1909, was very timely. The new century had barely completed a decade and a sense of nationalist pride was developing in India. There were stirrings of a movement for freedom from foreign rule that was gathering momentum. Mahatma Gandhi's iconic book *Hind Swaraj* or Indian Home Rule, which he wrote in Gujarati, was published the same year. The English translation of *The Indian War of Independence of 1857* by Vinayak Damodar Savarkar also came out. Both books were banned by the

British government. Thus, the surge of excitement that the unearthing of an ancient, legendary text aroused, was just in tune with the prevailing political climate.

But what exactly is this legendary text, the Arthashastra, about? While the title literally translates as 'science of wealth', it can be better described as a treatise on the science of governance. *Artha*, or the pursuit of material gain or prosperity, is considered one of the four *purusharthas* or aims of life in Hindu philosophy. But the writings of the Arthashastra go far beyond that. This work contains almost everything possible about the art of efficiently administering a country.

It is generally accepted that the Arthashastra was compiled between the second and third century BCE and was not the work of a single individual. Written in Sanskrit, the language of scholars at the time, it consists of fifteen books containing 150 chapters and covering 180 topics. The second book is the lengthiest, with 1285 sentences, while the eleventh is the shortest, with just fifty-six sentences. The chapters are written mainly in prose but conclude with verses. This was the typical style followed in ancient Sanskrit texts.

Why is this old treatise considered so important, apart from its historical value? First, the fact that a work of such wide-ranging scope and vision was written in our country centuries ago demonstrates the quality of scholarship and discourse that had evolved in ancient India. Secondly, the vastness of this work is incredible—it covers almost every subject concerning governance in extensive detail. Thirdly, Kautilya shows an approach that is both practical and humanitarian. Lastly, this work provides us with valuable insights into the kind of society that existed in that era.

What are the main ideas that the Arthashastra covers? These extend from statecraft to economic policy to military strategy. Kautilya gave primary importance to *artha* or the financial aspect of governance. He also devised a bureaucratic system that addressed practically all the requirements of an efficient administration and a legal system that covered civil and criminal law. Topics such as the education of a future king, his duties, foreign policy, theories on war and peace, markets and trade all find a place in this text.

In addition, the Arthashastra deals with several aspects of social welfare and lays emphasis on dharma, or the code of ethics that binds society, following the traditions of Hindu philosophy.

While it discusses a monarchical system, the theories propounded in the Arthashastra can apply to almost any form of government.

We may well ask if all these ideas about statecraft were derived from actual practice. There is good reason to believe that Kautilya employed his theories as prime minister under Chandragupta Maurya, the first emperor of India and laid the foundations of a well-governed empire. The Mauryan empire continued to expand and prosper till the reign of Chandragupta's grandson Ashoka the Great, and we can well assume that these principles of administering a country, its foreign policy, revenue collection and military strategy contributed immensely to its success.

The Arthashastra is an ancient text. Then how can it be considered relevant in contemporary times? Apart from the fact that Kautilya talked about a monarchical system of government, all the other theories of administration, law and order, taxes, social welfare, trade, defence and diplomacy that he proposed are universal and timeless. Indeed, the Arthashastra has been accorded an important place among classic works on the science of government. It has a pragmatic but thoughtful approach to governance. Kautilya declared, 'the ultimate source of the prosperity of the kingdom is its security and the prosperity of its people'. Like the modern welfare state, the Arthashastra displays concern for the common man, the less privileged sections of society, the weak and the elderly and even animals.

Interestingly, Kautilya's interpretation of the three aims of human existence—dharma, artha and kama—differed from that of other philosophers of his time. The general belief was that all three should be given equal importance, as giving too much importance to one would create a disbalance. Kautilya, however, placed artha or economics, above the others and claimed that the other two could not be practised effectively if artha was not placed foremost.

For these reasons, to this day, the Arthashastra is consulted, quoted and held up as a manual for good governance. *Chanakya Neeti*, a widely circulated compilation of his principles, is extremely popular, too.

WHO WAS KAUTILYA?

Many scholars acknowledge Kautilya as the author of the Arthashastra, or at least the compiler. However, there are disagreements over whether Kautilya is the same man known as Chanakya, who was responsible for bringing Chandragupta Maurya to power in Magadha. The whole issue hinges around the date of the composition of the treatise and the fact that no historical evidence has been found about the existence of a minister named Kautilya at the Mauryan court.

Chandragupta ascended the throne sometime between 321 and 325 BCE. Much of the information about his reign has been gathered from *Indica*, the account left by Megasthenes, the Greek ambassador of Seleucos Nikator, one of Alexander the Great's generals who took charge of some of Alexander's territories after his death. There is no mention of Kautilya or Chanakya in *Indica*. However, this text is also lost, and its existence is known only through references in the works of later historians.

Most of what we know about Kautilya comes from the accounts in Buddhist and Jain texts. What we can gather from these is that Kautilya's given name was Vishnugupta. Since he was the son of a Brahmin called Chanak, he came to be known as Chanakya. The other name of Kautilya was used because he belonged to the Kutila gotra. The legend goes that he was born with a full set of teeth, which was believed to foretell that he was destined for kingship. Uneasy about this possible future of a Brahmin child, Chanakya's parents decided to break the ill-omened teeth. Chanakya grew up to be a great scholar and gained mastery over the Vedas. He became a teacher at the famous University of Taxila. Once, when he heard that King Dhana Nanda of Magadha was organizing an assembly of learned Brahmins, he decided to join it and demonstrate his knowledge. Unfortunately, it is said that he was insulted by the king for occupying a seat that was not meant for him. Furious, Chanakya untied his *shikha* or topknot and vowed not to tie it up again till he had executed his revenge on Dhana Nanda.

There are different versions of his meeting with Chandragupta Maurya as well. The most popular one says that when he left Pataliputra after the episode at Dhana Nanda's court, he came across a group of children playing the game of kingship. The young Chandragupta was enacting the role of the king. Intrigued, Chanakya stopped to watch. When he observed how confidently the boy conducted himself and passed judgement, he was extremely impressed. He even tested him by posing as a poor Brahmin in need of alms and Chandragupta solemnly presented him with a stick as a make-believe cow. It struck him that this child possessed great potential and he could use him to further his plans of revenge on Dhana Nanda. On making enquiries, he learned that a hunter had found this boy as a baby and was bringing him up as his own son. After some discussion, Chandragupta's adoptive parents agreed to let Chanakya take their son under his wing and educate him. Some accounts claim Chanakya paid them 1000 *karshapanas*, the coins used that time, as compensation. He took the boy to Taxila where he trained him in various arts. Chandragupta proved to be a quick learner, justifying Chanakya's instinctive assessment.

The silver *karshapana*, usually known as *pana* was the prevalent coin of that period. Most panas weighed 3.4 gms.

Chanakya now began to look for allies who would assist Chandragupta and him in a campaign against the Nanda king and was able to raise an army. Their first attempt to conquer Magadha was unsuccessful. However, after Chanakya changed his strategy and attacked the kingdom from its outer areas, he was able to vanquish Dhana Nanda and place his protégé on the throne of Magadha. Chanakya is said to have played an important role in guiding Emperor Chandragupta Maurya as his prime minister.

THE ARTHASHASTRA

CHAPTER 1

ALL ABOUT KINGSHIP

In Kautilya's times, monarchy was the predominant system of government. Dynastic rule was the norm but not necessarily guaranteed. Since kings often exerted absolute power, it was crucial that a ruler be an intelligent, considerate and compassionate individual who put the welfare of his subjects foremost. He also needed to be courageous and well-trained in the martial arts because he had to lead his troops while defending his realm or conquering new territories.

Today, monarchy is considered an outdated concept of government, though a few countries still have kings and queens who play a ceremonial role more because their people are sentimental about such institutions, like in the UK. Norway, Sweden, Denmark and Thailand also have similar constitutional monarchies. In contrast, in Saudi Arabia, Oman and Swaziland, the monarch wields absolute power even now. But in most parts of the world, the democratic process of electing a government headed by a leader, the prime minister or president, is the norm.

Elected leaders are mostly individuals who have been successful in the world of politics because of their charisma and leadership qualities. There is no such thing as training to be the ruler of a country. This is because in a democracy, the leader and their party acquire power through their own skills in convincing voters that they are the right people for the job.

Kautilya, however, believed that a future king needed the best training possible.

A KING'S TRAINING

Kautilya gave utmost importance to the trained intellect and self-discipline of a ruler. The Arthashastra goes into detail about the education of a future king, and emphasis is placed on discipline. This discipline is interpreted as: obeying your teacher, having an interest in acquiring knowledge but also the mental capacity to understand what you are taught and absorb it, and pondering over what you have studied and interpreting its meaning. He defined discipline as being of two kinds—inborn and acquired. According to him, only those who possessed the qualities of natural self-control could derive maximum benefit from training. Also, the rule of law, which was essential to guaranteeing the security and welfare of the people depended on the ruler's moral fibre.

Kautilya further said that an individual who was deficient in intelligence would not be able to gain knowledge from even the best teacher.

> The fascinating story about the creation of the Panchatantra tales demonstrates the importance given to the proper training of princes. A king was in despair because his three sons were so dull that they could not learn anything. A man named Vishnusharma took on the challenge and made up these stories to teach them about the art of intelligent living. Since then, these stories have become a classic known worldwide.

A specific course of education was prescribed for princes who might ascend a throne one day. It included studying under noted gurus in an ashram to master the Vedas and philosophy and learn about the art of government from exponents of statecraft as well as politicians who had practical experience.

> In the Ramayana, Rama and his brothers studied the Vedas under Guru Vashishtha and learnt the martial arts from Guru Vishwamitra.

The ashrama period was known as the Brahmacharya stage, after which Kautilya recommended marriage at the age of sixteen. However, he emphasized that learning should continue in the form of association with scholarly people.

He laid out a routine for a prince to follow, which in some ways is not so different from a school timetable and also includes what you might describe as homework!

The first part of the day was to be devoted to practising the martial arts. This meant working with elephants, horseback riding, chariot racing and acquiring adeptness in warfare on foot. Mastery in the use of all kinds of weapons was essential. The second part of the day was to be spent listening to the *Itihasas*. The final part of the day was for examining the lessons for the next day, going over the ones studied earlier and listening repeatedly to points which had not been clear. It is believed that Chandragupta Maurya went through this rigorous training at the University of Takshashila.

The Itihasas are said to be written accounts of important events from the ancient past. The Ramayana, Mahabharata and the Puranas are among the important Itihasas. They were usually narrated by bards.

Kautilya identified lust, anger, greed, conceit, arrogance and recklessness as the six enemies that lead to the downfall of kings and gave the examples of Ravana and Duryodhana, who were destroyed by such vices. Kautilya claimed that the right training would help a king acquire control over his senses and avoid this fate.

The *Rajrishi* or wise, sage-like king is held up as an example of the ideal ruler who has mastered his senses and adheres to all the principles of dharma.

However, this does not mean a king should deprive himself of worldly pleasures. He simply should not fall prey to self-indulgence and let his weaknesses overpower him to the extent that he neglects his duties.

A KING'S DUTIES

Kautilya believed that the ideal king was energetic and hardworking. An indolent monarch would set a bad example for his people. When the people of a country developed slothful habits, the revenue would be depleted, creating a shortage of funds. Without money to support an efficient army, the king could easily be overcome by his enemies.

Thus, Kautilya prepared a demanding timetable for a king's daily routine, and his methods of time management were interesting.

What was this timetable? The conscientious ruler was to divide his day into eight periods of one and a half hours each to enable him to tackle all his tasks efficiently.

At dawn, he was to circumambulate a cow, its calf and a bull and then proceed to court.

For the first one and a half hours after daybreak, he should receive reports on defence, revenue and state expenditures.

The second one and a half hours would be devoted to public audiences and entertaining the petitions of his people.

The next one and a half hours were for personal activities, like taking a bath, having a meal and studying.

In the next period, before noon, the king was advised to accept revenue and tributes, attend to the appointment of ministers and high officials and assign their duties.

One and a half hours after noon were meant to be devoted to writing letters and dispatches, discussions with councillors and the important task of going through the reports of spies.

The next period was allotted as personal time—for recreation or reflection.

The subsequent one and a half hours were to be spent inspecting the armed forces.

In the period before sunset, the king was to confer with the chief of defence on matters concerning the security of the country.

Then, it was time for evening prayers. However, the king's duties did not end after sunset.

For the first one and a half hours after sunset, he would receive his secret agents for updates.

A second personal period followed—for a bath, a meal and study.

At 9 p.m., the king was to go to his bedchamber and accompanied by the sound of music, sleep for four and a half hours.

He would be woken to the sound of music again and spend the next one-and-a-half-hour period contemplating political issues and mulling over the tasks to be attended to.

The next period would be spent in discussion with his councillors and in sending out spies.

Then, another one and a half hours before sunrise were to be spent on his religious and household affairs, consulting his teacher, his purohit and his adviser on rituals, his personal physician, his astrologer and his head cook.

Thus, the king had to maintain a far more gruelling routine than his subjects. He was allowed only ten and a half hours of personal time, of which four and a half were for sleeping. This sounds almost as if a king was expected to be a superhero!

He was also counselled to be available to supplicants and not keep people waiting at the door. If he did not interact personally with his people, it would impact his decision-making, lead to disaffection and his people could go over to the enemy. This shows that Kautilya's ideal king had to be conscious of public opinion.

THE KING'S SECURITY

We are familiar with the saying, 'Uneasy lies the head that wears the crown.' Heads of state today are surrounded by heavy security. The king too, always had to be on his guard—against assassination attempts, palace coups by ambitious people and the threat of territorial expansion from neighbouring rulers. Chandragupta Maurya is said to have occupied a different bedroom each night to protect himself. There is also the story that Chanakya tried to make him immune to poison by adding small quantities of it to his food, which led to the tragic death of his wife, Durdara, when she ate from his thali.

Keeping this in mind, Kautilya began the Arthashastra by offering detailed instructions about the construction of the king's palace. A suitable site was to be chosen after consulting specialists in the art of architecture. The buildings were to be secured from attacks by constructing fortifications all around, which had to be heavily guarded. The palace complex would possess several halls as required. The king's personal apartments were to be placed in the centre, with emergency exits in case of attack. If we compare the plans of these palaces with that of high-security buildings in modern times, it would seem that many ideas have been borrowed from this ancient text.

The Arthashastra has several suggestions for the construction of concealed escape routes, which seem extremely elaborate and could fox the most cunning enemy. Some of these are:

◉ An underground treasury consisting of three floors
◉ Hidden passages inside walls
◉ A cellar with a secret stairway inside the walls that leads to the king's room. There should be a tunnel leading to a strategically placed temple with a wooden image of a god concealing the exit.
◉ An escape route through the upper floors via a staircase hidden inside the walls or a pillar or under a trap door

The apartments of the queens were to be built directly behind the king's residence, along with the maternity ward and infirmary. They would be surrounded by ponds and trees. The dwellings of the princes and princesses would be behind these.

Various other chambers, essential for life in the palace, were part of this plan. The precise locations of the council hall, the audience hall, the hall where the princes were to do their lessons, the guards' quarters and the kitchen and stores are mentioned. Heavily armed guards would be on duty between the buildings and movement within the palace complex was to be more regulated than in the strictest student hostels of today. None of the residents were permitted to move from their allotted chambers to stay in those meant for others. They were also not allowed to mingle with outsiders. Any object entering the king's household was to be scrutinized thoroughly, and the time of its arrival was noted. It could only proceed further after the seal of approval had been put on it.

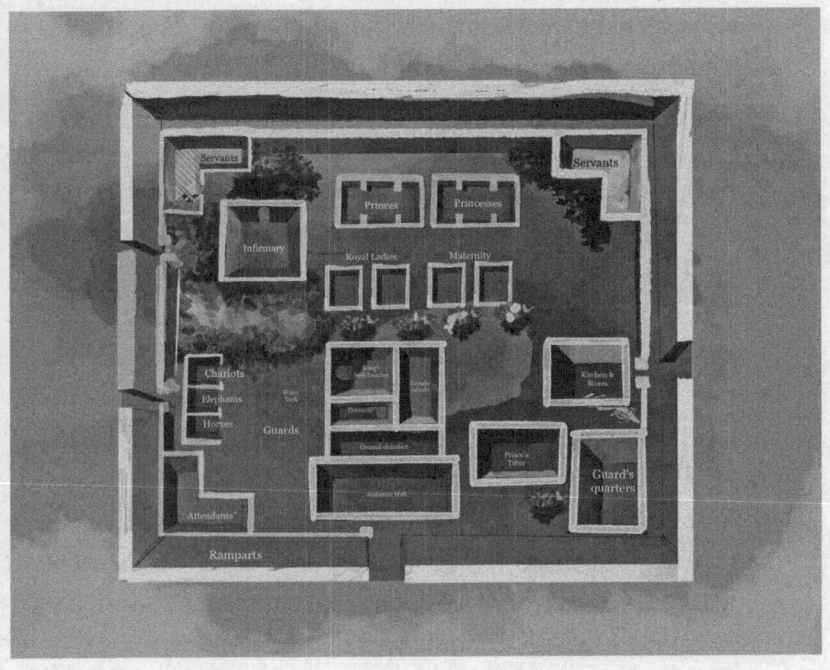

Kautilya had also considered other dangers that could be life-threatening. To prevent snake bites, plants that snakes avoid were to be grown around the palace and animals and birds like mongooses and peacocks were to be let loose on the ground. Birds that sound alarms against poisonous species, like parrots, shrikes, herons and partridges, were also to be kept.

Speed breakers and concealed traps were to be placed at strategic points to prevent ill-intentioned people from entering.

While the king was asleep in his bedchamber, his female guard of archers guarded him from the confines of an adjacent chamber. After he awoke, he was attended to by eunuchs. Then he would meet dwarfs, hunchbacks and *kiratas*, probably as an auspicious beginning to the day. Finally, he would enter his council hall to confer with the ministers and his relatives. Guards bearing spears would always man the doors.

For additional safety, Kautilya advised that the king employ only those whose loyalty was beyond doubt as personal attendants.

The threat of poisoning loomed constantly over the king. For this reason, the kitchen was also to be well guarded and its location kept secret. The head cook's job was to ensure that fresh and tasty food was served to the monarch. The king was to first offer food to a special fire and give some to the birds before eating his meal. Kautilya also provided methods of recognizing the presence of poison—whether in food, water, or wine, even on bed sheets, metals and gems. He warned that a person who was behaving suspiciously could well be a poisoner.

Many details for vetting the people serving the ruler are provided. These servers were to maintain strict personal hygiene, and each object that the king used had to be properly scrutinized. Similarly, a strict code was to be enforced on entertainers and musicians. Their musical instruments had to be stored in the palace, including the decorations of their elephants, saddles for horses, etc.

The measures for the king's safety extended to all his activities. He could swim only if crocodiles and dangerous fish had been removed from the water and enter a park only after it had been checked for snakes. He could not even go hunting unless the forest had been sanitized—checked for robbers, wild animals and enemies.

When inspecting his troops the king was advised to be well-armed, mounted on a horse, chariot or elephant. When he left his palace, guards bearing arms or truncheons would flank the roads, which would be cleared in advance. The king was not to enter a crowd or even a fair or festival without security.

Citing examples of queens who had assassinated their consorts, Kautilya in his book warned the monarch to be cautious even in his interactions with his queen. He advised the king to visit her in her own chambers only after a proper inspection. The queen was forbidden to entertain outsiders. Even her family members could visit her only when she had given birth or was ill. All her attendants would be vetted by spies.

If the queen could pose a danger, what about the princes, who stood to gain most in the event of their father's death? Kautilya quoted the opinions of different thinkers on this subject who believed that the king's sons had to be treated like potential enemies.

Kautilya believed that a son should not be considered a threat. Instead, he should be encouraged to assimilate the real meaning of dharma and artha and learn to discriminate between right and wrong conduct. As he grew older, he was to only keep company with right-minded people who would steer him away from bad habits and influence him to stay loyal to his father.

To maintain the high status of the monarch, stringent punishments were advised for those disrespecting the king, inciting rebellion or misusing his property. These were quite severe—amputation, death by impalement, being boiled alive—and may seem barbarous by contemporary standards. These horrific penalties were no doubt meant to drive home the fact that the king was all powerful.

At the same time, Kautilya cautioned the king about his personal conduct. If the king indulged in excessive drinking and other dissolute practices, he would lose the respect of his people, which could lead to unrest and instability.

AGAINST REVOLTS, REBELLIONS, CONSPIRACIES AND TREASON

The king was vulnerable to the conspiracies of ambitious people who coveted his position. The threat could be from someone close to him, like his queen or his sons. It could be from the chief priest or purohit, or his ministers, the general of his army, a power-hungry army commander in a distant part of his kingdom, a tribal chief or the king of a country subservient to him. It could also be a lone enemy or a group plotting against him, perhaps instigated by an enemy ruler who promised to reward them. A revolt by a disaffected segment of the people was possible too especially when the king was away on a military campaign, leaving the capital to his deputies. An impoverished and deprived people could attempt to improve their lives by seeking out an enemy ruler or rebelling against the king.

Kautilya recommended the organization of an efficiently run intelligence network to keep treachery at bay by sniffing it out in advance. Spies were to circulate among the people in disguise and report any signs of dissatisfaction. Malcontents were to be closely watched.

Kautilya provided a list of reasons why the public might get disenchanted with their ruler as a caution in the Arthashastra. Most of these reasons were failures of adherence to the accepted moral code as well as errors of judgement. The ruler was advised not to favour wrongdoers over deserving people and mete out unjust punishment. He needed to be particular about fulfilling his promises to the people and not squander public funds. Once again, the Arthashastra emphasizes correct conduct on the part of the ruler, fulfilling his responsibilities sincerely, respecting his advisers and appreciating and rewarding deserving individuals.

Kautilya analyzed the different kinds of revolts to provide specific guidelines for the ruler. According to him, when a king was about to set out on a campaign, he was particularly vulnerable. A rebellion in the capital city or central regions could be led, as earlier mentioned, by the crown prince, his purohit, a minister or the general of the army. If it occurred in the outer regions of his territory, it could be a local chief, the commander of a border post, a jungle chief or a defeated king under his hegemony.

Kautilya considered internal rebellion the most dangerous kind because it usually involved trusted people close to the ruler. Kautilya's view was that a revolt by the ministers of the court was the worst, and he advised the king to keep both the treasury and the army under his direct and rigorous control.

Kautilya suggested certain measures to stave off rebellion. If the king was leaving on a campaign and had reason to doubt an individual's loyalty, he was advised to take him along as a hostage. If he suspected that there could be a revolt on the borders, he should take the wife and children of the likely traitor.

According to Kautilya, it was not advisable to go on a military expedition while trouble was brewing within the country. If the revolt was a fallout of the king's bad policies, then he needed to set them right. If it was because of another person's ambition, the king needed to mete out exemplary punishment.

In case the ruler was in a vulnerable position and unable to recover lost territory from a rebel, Kautilya advised him to negotiate and let the rebel retain his winnings to prevent him from teaming up with a neighbouring ruler. The king was also asked to instigate such a ruler or a jungle chief to attack the rebel. While the rebel would be preoccupied fighting them off, the king was to use the opportunity to make a strike. The king could also create disaffection within the enemy's stronghold to weaken him.

In the case of revolts by ministers or the army chief, Kautilya advocated parley as the first resort. But if that did not work, the other options suggested could be tried.

When the governor of a province, a jungle chieftain or a vassal king rose against the ruler to seek independence, Kautilya suggested that another king, a chieftain or a disaffected prince or kinsman was to be instigated to attack this person. Alternatively, there could be negotiations. Secret agents could also be deployed to create a rift in case the rebel teamed up with an enemy. If the rebel backtracked and parted company with the enemy, he was to be rewarded; otherwise, the secret agent was to offer incentives to the rebel's own accomplices to kill him.

Kautilya also classified the different kinds of revolts in order of gravity, placing a revolt in the interior instigated by conspirators located in the centre of the kingdom in the most dangerous category. The revolts in the outer regions of the country, plotted by men in either the outer regions or inner ones, were in the second category, and the remedy advised was to create dissension and use force. The least threatening was the revolt at the centre instigated by distantly placed rebels and here he suggested reconciliation and gifts. For the most dangerous one, all methods were to be employed to crush it.

WHO WOULD BE THE NEXT KING?

The question of succession was another crucial aspect of kingship. Kautilya asserted that only a person with royal blood would find ready acceptance from the public. A commoner aspiring to kingship, even if he possessed sterling leadership qualities, might be rejected.

Normally, the eldest son would succeed his father unless he was mentally or physically unfit or possessed such qualities of character that disqualified him. In this event, the king was to designate one of his other sons. If the king had only one son and that son was unsuitable to be a ruler, he was not to be placed on the throne under any circumstances. In such a situation, joint rule by members of the royal family or, in other words, an oligarchy, was suggested to maintain law and order and proper governance.

According to Kautilya, there were three kinds of sons. The wise son would grasp the importance of dharma and artha during his education and apply these principles in his life. The lazy son was one who would understand these principles but not take the trouble to follow them. The wicked son was the one who abhorred the practice of dharma and artha and rejected them, giving himself over to immoral ways. Such a son was never to be designated as the heir apparent. Instead, his son or a daughter's deserving son was to be declared as the crown prince.

The princes were to be watched constantly by members of the secret service. In case they displayed signs of disaffection, they were to be sent to distant regions where there was no danger of their creating a power centre or fomenting rebellion. If a prince was disgruntled but otherwise worthy, he was to be appointed to an important position, like chief of defence, or declared heir apparent to prevent him from revolting. If an only son to whom the

Chandragupta Maurya's son Bindusara apparently appointed his son Ashoka (the Great) as the governor of Ujjaini to keep him out of the way. Similarly, Shahjahan sent Aurangzeb to administer the Deccan. In both cases, these strategies rebounded on the father.

father was deeply attached showed signs of staging a coup, he was to be imprisoned.

Kautilya was aware that a deserving prince might be treated unfairly by his father. His advice for the prince was to obey his father, except when he was assigned duties that put his life in danger, make him unpopular with the people or if he was expected to commit an evil act.

While Kautilya gave a lot of importance to dharma, he justified and advised what we might consider unethical behaviour on the part of a prince who had been treated unfairly by his father. For example, Kautilya said that such a prince could resort to robbery to raise funds, make friends with members of heretical groups, rich widows or traders and steal their gold, silver and precious stones to support himself or fund a rebellion against his father. He could also seek the support of his mother's relatives to fight his father and even plan to assassinate him.

> The Mughal emperor Jahangir revolted against his father Akbar but was later pardoned. Jahangir's son Khusrau rebelled against him, and when he was defeated, Jahangir imprisoned him and had him partially blinded. He regretted it later and tried to find cures but was unsuccessful.

As for the father, when a king found that a son was discontented and could stage a coup, Kautilya suggested that the king coax him to return. If he refused, the king could either have him assassinated or use trickery to arrest and imprison him.

The succession was to be decided in an orderly manner, whether the king had died on the battlefield or of illness in the palace. In the case of a minor prince, the most senior person in the council of ministers was to take charge and act as regent. The office of Chief Councillor is not mentioned in the Arthashastra, so it could be the eldest or most experienced among them.

If the king fell victim to a life-threatening illness, the councillors were to take certain measures to guarantee a smooth succession in order to preserve peace and stability in the country.

When a king was seriously ill, visitors were to be restricted, and the news that he was extremely busy performing rituals for the welfare of the country was to be circulated. A body double could also be employed to lull suspicion.

Measures were to be taken to ensure that no disturbances occurred in case news of the king's illness leaked out. The councillor was advised to secure the treasury and the army in one place, either within the fort or in a safe spot on the frontier. The princes, close relatives and high officials were also to be summoned. If there were indications that the commander of a fort or a jungle chieftain was becoming hostile, he would be placated, sent off on a risky campaign or asked to visit a friend of the king.

Action was to be taken against any neighbouring ruler who tried to exploit the situation. He could be tricked into visiting the kingdom and then coerced into making a treaty or be executed.

Kautilya advised a swift transition of power. The support of the princes, the king's other relations and the high-ranking officials was to be elicited to announce that the chosen heir had been crowned, even if the king was not already dead.

After putting the crown prince in charge, the councillor was to announce the illness of the king and manage affairs of state with a firm hand to ensure the security of the country.

If a king died in battle, especially if he fell in hostile territory, the councillor was advised to parley with the enemy and then make a swift retreat. An ally pretending to be an enemy could help negotiate beneficial terms. Else, the councillor could place a neighbouring ruler, who was an ally, on the throne and then retreat from the battle. Or he could immediately crown the chosen successor and continue the war.

When Emperor Qin Shi Huangdi of China died in 210 BCE, he was hundreds of miles away from home. His advisers wanted to keep his death a secret till they returned to the capital and told everyone that he was sleeping in his carriage. His meals were delivered, messages continued to be sent in his name and questions were answered. To conceal the smell of his decaying body, a cartload of rotting fish was made to accompany his carriage.

If the heir to the throne was too young or there was no heir, Kautilya advised the councillor to crown any prince, be it the king's brother or a son who was unsuitable. The councillor could even enthrone a princess or a pregnant queen. All the important officials would be exhorted to support the new ruler, saying that he was only a symbol and they would hold the reins of government. Then, with the backing of the supporters who would insist that the councillor was the only person efficient enough to administer the kingdom, he could be appointed regent. The salaries of the councillors who supported this councillor's regency would be increased, as would those of the armed forces. As regent, the councillor would fulfil all the duties of a ruling monarch. He would also bear the responsibility of educating the young prince in a suitable manner. If there was no young prince or pregnant queen, the princess was to be married to an appropriate man, and her son was to be groomed to be the future king.

When the young prince reached the age when he could govern independently, the regent was to request retirement. If the king insisted that he stay on, he could continue to guide him; otherwise, he was to retire to the forest but appoint a group of trustworthy men to guard and advise the king.

Women rulers seem to be unknown in Kautilya's time. However, girls received an education, and women scholars took part in philosophical debates and became teachers. Some of them, known as *brahmavadinis*, did not marry and pursued learning all their lives. The king had female guards and women soldiers in his army. They also participated in sports. Women possessed property rights and marriage laws were fair to them: divorce and widow remarriage was permitted.

THE INCOMPETENT RULER

Kautilya believed that an uneducated ruler could be guided by wise councillors, but one who had immoral inclinations would always do as he pleased and plunge the country into a ruinous course.

If a king was in poor health, would he abdicate? Kautilya felt that the ruler should continue to perform his duties as best as possible. It would be better than allowing another king to seize his throne. A usurper would not be sympathetic to the people and a tyrannical rule could lead to unrest, anarchy and his eventual overthrow.

In this way, almost all the facets of kingship and challenging situations concerning it were minutely examined in the Arthashastra and suggestions were made for the most efficient practices.

CHAPTER 2

WHAT IS A WELL-ORGANIZED STATE?

The contemporary world may have advanced in numerous ways over the centuries, but the basics of good governance remain the same as in the times of the Arthashastra. Countries with well-functioning administrative systems, effective enforcement of law and order and policies that guarantee the welfare of all their citizens thrive and provide a decent quality of life for their people.

Kautilya gave much weight to the organization of the state in such a manner that it was effectively protected against hostile forces and remained prosperous through the dedicated pursuit of agriculture and trade. He provided instructions to accomplish this in minute detail, attending to almost every aspect of administering a country. He also believed that the maintenance of the law and proper governance would ensure the welfare of the public. A new king might inherit either an efficient or faulty system, but it was for him to make reforms as required. Such a ruler might be ambitious to conquer new territory, but Kautilya felt that it was essential to first put a well-oiled administration in place lest the kingdom fell apart in his absence.

The Arthashastra considers these among the most important features of the *janapada* meaning state or countryside, the fortified city and the governing officials.

Kautilya believed that the land was the source of sustenance for the country and the key to its well-being. The wise ruler paid attention to the following aspects—fertile land that could be cultivated for pastures, forests where elephants lived (elephants played a crucial role in military operations) and forests for timber, forts, frontier posts, roads and trade routes. These were to be efficiently organized and administered by suitable officials.

NEW SETTLEMENTS

Kautilya recommended that, first, a new ruler should examine the condition of agricultural land since the countryside was the engine of economic activity. The ruler was advised to populate the uninhabited parts of the country by establishing new villages and reviving those abandoned for whatever reason. This could be accomplished by moving people from other parts to these areas or inviting foreigners to settle there. They could be offered incentives or even brought there by force.

These settlements were to be situated in such a manner that they provided protection to each other in case of enemy attacks or any other disaster. The boundaries were to be clearly laid out and were to be of one or two *krosas*—a measure of land equal to 3.66 kilometres. They were to be distinctly defined using natural features like rivers, mountains, a forest, a dry river bed, a cave, an embankment or trees like the silk cotton, acacia and milk tree.

While planning these settlements, the king was to be careful not to place them in a territory vulnerable to the enemy or jungle tribes. Neither were they to be located in areas prone to disease or famine. Kautilya also specified the rules for land grants to various segments of society.

A system of protection was to be established, with fortresses commanded by frontier chiefs on the borders, to guard entry into the kingdom. Additionally, a second layer of defence was to be implemented by allocating the forested area between the forts and villages to trappers, archers, hunters and forest tribes. Once the village was properly settled, much the way officials receive government accommodation today, land was to be allotted to the heads of departments, accountants, recordkeepers (*gopas*), divisional officers (*sthanika*), doctors, couriers and horse trainers. This land was to be granted only for the duration of their job. They were not permitted to sell or mortgage it.

When a new village was being settled, the farmers were to be given grants of grain, cattle and money as loans to be repaid later. They would also receive incentives and tax breaks, much like farmers receive free electricity and tax benefits in our country in present times. Further grants could be provided if it was felt that the farmers would increase revenue and prevent losses to the treasury. The king was to be paternal towards his subjects and not be harsh on those who could not make good on their exemptions.

Kautilya advised that these villages should be developed in fertile areas where water for irrigation was available and it was possible to produce two crops in a year. There should be elephant forests and trade routes nearby to transport the produce. If the area was uncultivable, it could be sold and taken back when the buyer failed to produce anything from it.

Actors, singers, storytellers, musicians and minstrels were to be discouraged from entering these settlements. There were to be no distractions that prevented the tillers from producing as much grain and other commodities as they could.

It sounds rather harsh that people were not to be allowed any entertainment as a relief from their work. But we must remember that Kautilya was talking about the ideal state where every citizen was employed in productive activity to contribute to the state exchequer.

Promoting economic activity

For Kautilya, economic activity was the key to the power of a king and the welfare of the public. Without the backing of a strong economy, a king would be vulnerable to attack from other rulers because he would lack the means to defend the country. This wealth, as earlier mentioned, came from the countryside and every attempt was to be made to encourage and support agriculture. Farmers were to be protected from harassment, and taxes and fines were to be reasonable. Also, farmers were not to be drafted as labour for state projects.

Forts were to be constructed to provide shelter to the people in case of an enemy attack or in the event of natural disasters, reservoirs were to be built to supply water for agriculture and trade routes were to be maintained because they fulfilled many purposes—the coming and going of secret agents and transporting of war material. Mines had to be kept in proper order since they supplied metals to forge arms along with precious metals and gems. Forest produce was to be given proper value and all kinds of forests were to be preserved. In this sense, Kautilya provided a practical reason for saving the environment. He also mentioned animal sanctuaries, either near the border or at any other suitable spot where animals could be protected.

Reservoirs were to be kept well supplied with water from natural springs or other places. Individuals who constructed storage reservoirs would be given aid in the form of land for constructing roads and channels for water, as well as timber and other tools.

Shrines and sanctuaries were to be provided with similar support.

Interestingly, the fish, ducks and vegetables produced would be the property of the king. He was to grant land for pastures in areas deemed unfit for farming. The cattle herds had to be given state protection from thieves, wild animals, poisonous creatures and disease.

A part of the forest was to be maintained for the king's recreation, in other words, for hunting or pleasure parties. It is worth noting that forests are highly valued in the Arthashastra. There is special mention of 'elephant forests', which were to be situated on the border of the kingdom under the supervision of the Chief Elephant Forester. The forests were to be demarcated according to the kind of produce they yielded, whether it was timber or different varieties of plants. There would be settlements of foresters near the woods to maintain them, and factories to process the produce were to be set up.

Trade routes were also to be protected. Courtiers, state officials and forest guards could not harass travellers. The roads had to be kept safe from thieves. Even herds of cattle were not allowed on them, lest they caused damage.

To encourage civic sense, citizens who contributed to public service by building embankments, bridges or beautified their villages were to receive incentives.

The Capital City

The Capital was to be established in the centre of the country on a site selected by construction experts. The confluence of two rivers was a highly recommended location. So was a site near a perennial lake or an artificial one fed by canals. Kautilya advised that the spot be well connected with both land and water trade routes and developed as a market town.

Details about the recommended construction of the city were given, which shows that Kautilya understood that proper town planning was essential for providing a good quality of life to the citizens. Cities were to be heavily fortified against enemy attack, and he suggested the city fort be surrounded by three moats. These moats were to have proper drainage and be filled with lotuses and crocodiles.

Further, it was advised to construct a stockade of bricks and stones—never wood as it was inflammable—eighteen to thirty-six feet high and nine to eighteen feet wide, on top of the earth rampart.

A detailed plan for the city was provided. The palace was to be in the centre and face either north or east. The centre of the city would also contain temples dedicated to Shiva, Lakshmi, Vaishravana, Aswin and Kali as well as shrines meant for the gods of victory. Temples of tutelary gods would be distributed through out the city and guardian gods would be enshrined at the four main gates.

There would be six royal roads intersecting the city—three running from east to west and three from

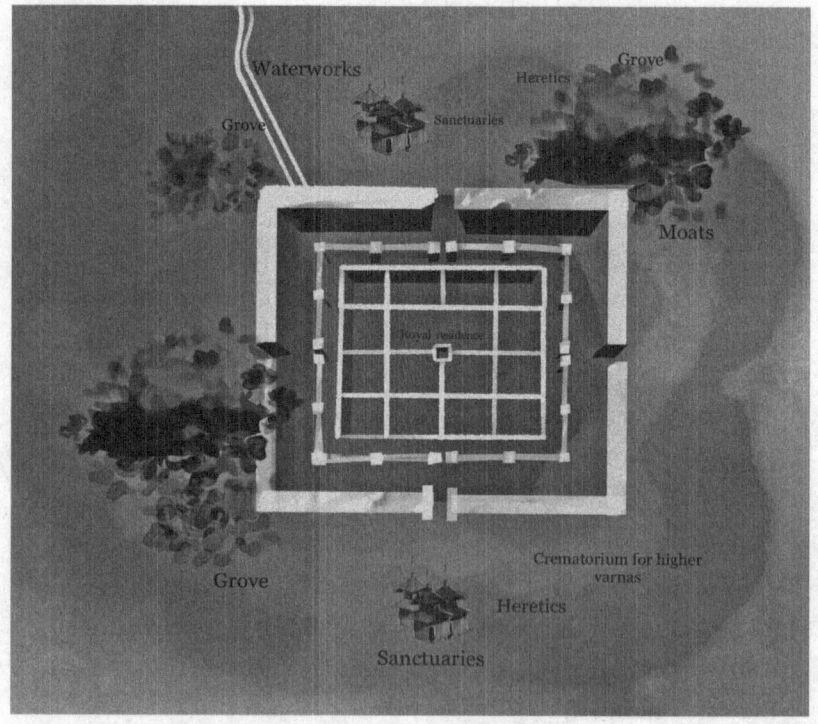

north to south. There would be twelve gates. Kautilya laid emphasis on proper water supply and drainage systems, as well as covered passages for convenience.

Sustainable livelihoods and civic amenities were given much importance. Thus, each household was to be provided with sufficient land. They could grow flowers and store grains as they needed. A well was to be dug to supply water to each group of ten houses.

It was also recommended that food supplies and other products of use be stored in a quantity sufficient for several years. These were to be replaced at appropriate intervals when they became stale.

THE ROYAL COUNCILLORS AND MINISTERS

The Arthashastra defines the business of government as threefold. One is the kind of work the king witnesses with his own eyes or supervises. The next is work that is reported to him. The third is tasks that have not been accomplished, which he must reason out from the information he possesses. Since the ruler could not oversee each and every government activity, he needed to appoint ministers to supervise different departments.

In contemporary times, we have a council of ministers who handle the different government departments. The royal councillors and ministers played a similar role. Given the responsibilities of their posts, these men had to be selected carefully.

In modern democracies, the leader of the party that wins the elections appoints the ministers. In ancient monarchies, it was the head of state who did this.

In our country, the President appoints the prime minister, who is the leader of the winning party. The President then appoints the other ministers on the advice of the prime minister. There are three categories in the council of ministers—cabinet ministers, ministers of state and deputy ministers. The cabinet ministers are the most important and are usually chosen for their electoral performance and superior abilities.

Kautilya offered certain suggestions about selecting the right people. Childhood friends were acceptable if they did not take advantage of their relationship with the king and stayed within their limits. Individuals whom the ruler trusted enough to share secrets with were also suitable as long as they did not try to exploit their relationship. The Arthashastra says that the loyal official should also be competent, the hereditary one should refrain from trying to get too much importance, and the new appointee should have both theoretical and practical knowledge of political life. The most important consideration was to appoint men who were above average in every way.

The Arthashastra advises the king not to undertake any task without due deliberation. These deliberations were to take place in secret and secluded place so that they remained confidential. Subsequently, a close watch was to be maintained on the participants, lest they reveal decisions taken on policy to the wrong people. Thus, officials and ministers were to remain under constant scrutiny. A close eye was to be kept on foreign envoys too.

Kautilya had clear views on how many people were to be involved in policy-making discussions. To maintain secrecy, the king was not to consult more than three or four of his advisers at a time and make his own decisions later. He could also seek guidance from each adviser separately and ask them to provide plausible reasons for it.

The role of the ministers

It is worth noting that the Arthashastra differentiates between ministers and councillors. The ministers were not necessarily the king's advisers. A few would enjoy this privilege, but the rest would actually be the officials who carried out the work. As Dr Kangle, the eminent translator mentions, this body was not 'a Cabinet armed with powers to enforce its decision on the King.'

The king was advised to select ministers according to their ability to perform a particular task. The number was to be decided according to the requirements of the government. Kautilya mentioned that Indra, the god, had a council of a thousand ministers who acted as his eyes and that is why he was known as the thousand-eyed one, though in reality he possessed only two eyes.

The ministers were to pay heed to the king's objectives while simultaneously keeping those of the enemy in mind. They were to continue working on old projects, make improvements on those that required them and begin new projects as needed. It was essential that they followed the king's orders faithfully.

The king was to confer with the ministers residing in the capital city, and he could correspond with those who were stationed in distant places. This differs from the modern concept of a minister living close to the seat of power. However, as elected representatives, today's ministers do visit their constituencies to attend to the needs of the public.

In an emergency, the king was supposed to summon both the group of councillors and the council of ministers to confer with them. He could follow the opinion of the majority but not take it as an absolute and use his own judgement to adopt the most suitable course of action.

Before appointment

In contemporary times, when an individual is under consideration for a sensitive public post—whether in the government, armed forces or judiciary—his or her background is investigated thoroughly. Kautilya had already envisioned this requirement in those ancient times and listed several points that needed to be verified before appointing a future minister. From his nationality and family background to his ability to maintain personal discipline, all these were to be substantiated by people who knew him well. Experts would examine him to determine his familiarity with various arts, and his intelligence, courage, and skill would be assessed on the basis of his earlier performance. His ability to think on his feet, his articulation, and his self-assurance would be tested in an interview. He would also be observed for his skill in interacting competently with different kinds of people, his fortitude in the face of adversity, his honesty, his trustworthiness and his sociability.

The king was to confer with his council and purohit before the appointment, and he had to use an appropriate person to test the candidate on the four heads of dharma, artha, kama and courage. During this test, attempts would be made to shake his loyalty on the grounds of religion, the promise of financial gain or inducements of the flesh, as well as by manipulating his fears.

The results of these tests would determine the line of work that would be allotted to each contender. Those who cleared the test of dharma were considered right for a post in the judiciary or law and order departments. Those who were proved incorruptible in the test of artha were suitable for the treasury as the chancellor or treasurer. Those who resisted the allure of worldly pleasures would be in charge of the department of recreation within and outside the palace. And those who proved to be courageous would receive duties near the person of the king. If a candidate passed every test successfully, he would be selected for the high position of chief councillor. Alternately, those who could not clear a single test would receive less desirable jobs in mines, forests, elephant forests or factories. Once the council of ministers was established, it was important for the king to organize his intelligence department according to his requirements.

The categories of officials

Each government needs a system of administration that ensures that the citizens can enjoy a certain level of comfort—sufficient nutrition and health care, adequate security, an assurance that they can pursue their professions without harassment and have access to means of entertainment during their leisure time.

In contemporary democracies, the prime minister heads the central government, there is a cabinet of ministers who advise him and different ministries that handle various departments. There is the parliament of elected representatives that makes the laws essential to a humane state that caters to all segments of society. While policies are framed by these bodies, it is the bureaucracy that executes the actual work of administration.

Thus, as earlier mentioned, the ruler was advised to hire knowledgeable and astute councillors whose opinions he valued and whom he trusted, along with a body of officials who would implement the policies this inner group decided upon efficiently.

While the king might be the leader, to a great extent, his authority depended on his individual abilities and his personality.

There have been rulers who managed to take complete charge of the government, like Louis XIV of France. He professed in 1661, 'L'etat est moi', or 'I am the state', and declared that he would not have any chief minister. Louis ushered in the Golden Age of France, but he was a rare individual.

It is interesting to note the official set up of the state as envisaged in the Arthashastra.

It does not seem very different from our contemporary system, which shows us how much this ancient work has contributed to the planning of modern governments.

What kind of job would you be eligible for if you lived in the times of Kautilya? If you did not possess a neat handwriting, there was no way you could aspire to the post of royal scribe, to give just one example.

If we examine the hierarchy of the officials according to their salaries, this is what we discover. The king is right on top, naturally, and in the rung below him are the *amatyas* or councillors, including the king's main councillors, four in number, one of whom served as the royal scribe, the *yuvaraj* or crown price, the *senapati* or chief of defence, the purohit, the *ritwik* or officiating priest and the acharya or the king's guru. All of them received a salary of 48,000 panas a year, a handsome amount that was expected to guarantee loyalty and prevent corruption. The queen mother and the head queen also received similar allowances. The raj purohit was selected for his knowledge of religious matters, political acumen and good judgement.

These were the top honchos as designated by Kautilya. No doubt Kautilya himself occupied the position of acharya or prime minister to Chandragupta Maurya. One rung lower in rank were the palace officials and those of the civil administration, who were to be given exactly half the salary—24,000 panas—which was expected to be sufficient to ensure their efficiency. There were eighteen categories of *mahamatras* as the top officials were known.

Among the important, highly paid palace officials were the *dauvarika* or king's chamberlain and the *antaravamsika* or the commandant of the palace guards. The dauvarika, or the doorkeeper, handed out the king's clothes to the valet and the required instruments to the barber, took care to see that the king was comfortable in every way and kept note of his schedule. The antaravamsika oversaw the king's appointments for the day and was like a personal secretary to the prime minister. There was also the *antaravamsikasainya*, the chief of the palace guards and even accompanied the king as his personal security officer when he was at war.

The *prasatr* received the same salary and appears to have been an official connected with the administration of the city or the judiciary. The *samnidhatra* or treasurer and the *samhartr* or chancellor were in the same rank. Both had to be men of impeccable honesty. In fact, Kautilya remarked that it was even more important for the chancellor to be upright than the treasurer because he could do more damage. While the role of the treasurer does not need much explanation, the chancellor, who seems to be the top official, supervised not only the department of revenue collection but also law and order and the secret service.

After the death of Aurangzeb, the Mughal empire began to disintegrate, and many provincial heads proclaimed themselves rulers. Even during Aurangzeb's rule and those of other strong monarchs, rebellions would frequently occur. Kautilya is very conscious of this danger. Thus, he recommended that the salary paid to the men who kept the state running smoothly and kept it safe from foreign invaders be fixed at an amount sufficient to keep them loyal. The *rashirapala* or governors of the provinces and particularly those that lay on the frontier, the *antapala*, had to be kept happy, lest they were tempted to break away and form their own governments. They were paid the sum of 12,000 panas a year. The *akshatpacalamadhyaksha* (a real mouthful!) corresponded to what we know as the chief controller and auditor, and we assume he received comparative emoluments.

No special foreign service existed. Envoys were selected from among the high-ranking officials.

HIERARCHY OF OFFICIALS AND SALARIES

THE KING

AMATYAS

- Royal scribe
- Crown prince
- Chief of defence
- Purohit
- Officiating priest
- King's guru

QUEEN MOTHER & HEAD QUEEN

RAJ PUROHIT (PRIME MINISTER)

48,000 panas

MAHAMATRAS
(PALACE OFFICIALS AND CIVIL ADMINISTRATION)

- Dauvarika (King's Chamberlain)
- Antaravamsika (Commandant of Palace Guards)
- Antaravamsikasainya (Chief of Palace Guards)
- Prasastr (City/Judiciary Administration)
- Samnidhatra (Treasurer)
- Samhartr (Chancellor)

24,000 panas

PROVINCIAL HEADS

- Rashirapala (Governors of the provinces)
- Antapala (Governers of the frontiers)

12,000 panas

Note: The salaries mentioned are in panas.

The Royal Scribe

A great deal of our historical information from ancient India is gathered from the edicts left on pillars and rocks. These edicts or royal proclamations were issued from time to time. They could be on a variety of subjects, from informative reports to commands on favours and punishments for the officers or awards granted. Kautilya attached great importance to the proper framing of edicts. He suggested a format which is quite similar to the one we use today, beginning with a salutation and ending with the name and title of the king.

The royal scribe was the officer in charge of these edicts, and he was expected to have a neat handwriting in the interest of clarity. If he wrote down an edict wrongly and it was proved that it was deliberate, he could be punished by cutting off both of his feet and hands, or he would have to pay a fine of 900 panas. We can say that the royal scribe was somewhat like a personal secretary to the king, noting down his commands and conveying them to the public.

The Treasurer

The treasurer managed the treasury and supervised the construction of public buildings, including warehouses, granaries and prisons. Specific plans were provided for each building, considering the size and perishability of the products. Measures such as rain gauges, wells and bathrooms were incorporated, along with security against rats and snakes using cats and mongooses. Shrines for guardian deities were also to be built. Additionally, a secret treasury was proposed for use during emergencies. The treasurer ensured the receipt of government property, ranging from timber to precious metals. Any actions causing loss to the treasury was punishable. The chief coin examiner verified coin authenticity, destroying counterfeits to prevent circulation.

The Chancellor

The chancellor collected revenue from the entire country, managed the settled areas (except fortified towns), maintained law and order and supervised the secret service. He prepared the budget, tracked revenue and expenses, aimed to increase revenue and decrease expenditure and maintained administration records. Governors oversaw cities under the chancellor's authority. The country was divided into provinces, each with a governor and record keepers for villages. Records detailed village classifications, tax status, contributions and land classifications. House numbering and resident records were recommended. Magistrates were appointed for tax collection oversight, and secret agents monitored public servants' performance. The chancellor also ensured efficient governance of the countryside.

The governor general of the city handled the administration of the city. His duties were similar to those of the chancellor, except that governing a city was different from managing the countryside. He was to divide the city into four parts and appoint a governor for each section.

The record keepers would maintain similar records of the population.

The density of the population and the needs of urban life required different kinds of laws. Thus, the governor general of the city was to:

- Maintain law and order, including the curfew regulations
- Keep control of trade—see that goods were sold at fair prices and check the sale of stolen goods
- Maintain sanitation and a clean environment, including the cremation grounds
- Ensure fire safety and fire-fighting equipment—it is interesting what measures have been suggested, which can be a lesson for our times. Those who worked with fire, like blacksmiths, were to occupy a different locality and inflammable material like thatch would be removed from there. Thousands of water jars were to be placed on the main roads, crossroads, city gates and all royal buildings.
- Control the prisons
- Keep custody of lost property

The official was to make daily inspections of water reservoirs, roads, drains, underground passages, ramparts and other fortifications.

The Chief Comptroller and Auditor

This official was to be responsible not only for the maintenance but also the construction of the Records Office. These records for different departments seem to be as detailed as the ones maintained in today's times.

Here again, inspectors were to be appointed in different grades and all the departments were to be under the constant watch of secret agents.

All the accounts were to be audited by audit officers.

Then, the comptroller and auditor would prepare a report for the king, which would include the estimated revenue, actual revenue, income expenditure and balance. He would also present the accounts of other officers and the activities of the government.

Frontier Officers

Frontier officers bore the responsibility of defending the borders and were to man the forts built at different entry points into the kingdom.

They would also levy and collect the road taxes, inspect the goods being transported by foreign caravans and assess their value. Another task of theirs was to pass on necessary information to the chief collector of customs.

In this manner, an efficiently designed system was envisaged for the orderly movement of merchandise. These officials had to ensure the safety of the goods being transported as well.

Thus, Kautilya covered almost all the aspects of a well-planned and efficient structure of governance, ranging from land usage and city planning to the hierarchy of officials who would handle the administration.

Keeping human fallibility in mind, the Arthashastra lists different categories of wrongdoers who stole public money and deprived the public of what was due to them. Secret agents would play a significant part in exposing such officials. They would either be fined or, if the offence was serious, sent into exile.

In addition, thieves, robbers, forest bandits and other criminals who were caught would be paraded in public to warn wrongdoers that they could not escape the king's ever watchful eye and escape punishment for their evil actions.

CHAPTER 3

HOW TO MAKE
A COUNTRY PROSPEROUS

Kautilya firmly believed that a sound economy ensured the welfare of a country and its inhabitants. Thus, he gave primary importance to those aspects that guaranteed it and advised the king to promote agriculture and industry as well as trade.

AGRICULTURE

When we examine Kautilya's theories on sound agricultural practices, we find they are broadly similar to the policies governments follow today. The land was to be classified according to the rainfall it received, which dictated the kinds of crops that could be grown there.

If you're thinking of going on a picnic, you'll probably check the weather forecast to see if it might rain before making plans. Thanks to the advancements in science and technology, today, we can get a reasonably accurate idea of the possibility of thundershowers or the daily temperature. But how did they predict the weather in those ancient times? Kautilya talks about different methods of rain forecasting by observing the heavenly bodies, like the position, movement and cloudiness of Jupiter, the setting and movement of Venus and variations in the appearance of the Sun. Studying Venus could indicate the amount of rainfall, the Sun could inform about the successful sprouting of seeds, and Jupiter could provide signs for the healthy growth of the plants.

Three clouds raining incessantly for seven days, eight clouds raining off and on and sixty clouds raining between periods of sunshine were considered indicators of beneficial rainfall.

Rain, sunshine and wind being dispersed in an appropriate ratio foretold a good harvest.

The method for preparing seeds and plants for sowing is also elaborated upon, as well as the seasons when they should be grown. This gives us a good idea of the kind of food people ate at the time. You might be surprised to learn that some of the grains, beans and pulses we consume today have been around since the Kautilyan era. Wheat, barley, varieties of millet and rice, lentils and beans, like whole or skinned urad dal, chana dal and horse gram, were popular. Yes, some version of dal makhani did exist then! Flax seeds are widely touted as a health food these days. At that time, they were commonly used along with other oilseeds, like mustard, sesame and safflower. Different kinds of root vegetables, gourds like pumpkins, and even sugar cane were cultivated in our country at that time. Ancient Indians enjoyed fruits like mangoes and grapes as well. A variety of medicinal plants and those used for making perfumes are also mentioned in the Arthashastra.

In today's times, farmers are given tax breaks and other incentives not only in India but also in other parts of the world. Kautilya, too, understood the importance of extending land under agriculture by advising that an individual who cultivated unfarmed land should be exempted from paying agricultural taxes for two years.

The necessity of constructing facilities for irrigation was also recognized with tax incentives for those who built new water tanks and embankments or repaired existing ones. Water conservation was given great importance, and people who wasted water or damaged water sources were to be punished or fined. People may complain about high water tax at times, but it is not a modern invention—it was levied in those ancient times too.

Today, we have several government schemes in India to promote agriculture. One such scheme is the National Mission for Sustainable Agriculture (NMSA), which has been formulated to enhance agricultural productivity, especially in rainfed areas, by focusing on integrated farming, water use efficiency, soil health management and synergizing resource conservation.

INDUSTRY

Industry and manufacturing are as essential to the well-being of any state as agriculture and trade. They supply products of use to consumers and provide employment and revenue to the government by way of taxes. Thus, modern-day governments have specific laws to regulate industries and also offer incentives to encourage them. This concept was well understood by Kautilya, and rules for promoting and regulating different kinds of industries were listed in the Arthashastra.

Which industries do you think existed in ancient India?

TEXTILES

How comfortable soft cotton fabrics feel against our skin in the blistering summer heat! They've been around for a long time in our country. The cultivation of cotton and the production of cotton fabric is believed to have originated in India, and it is likely that the spinning wheel was also invented here. As a result, we can conclude that the textile industry thrived during the Mauryan era. Apart from cotton, linen and silk were manufactured, too, and the process has been described in the Arthashastra. To encourage production, Kautilya suggested rewarding women engaged in spinning yarn and weavers, particularly those skilled in working with fine fabrics like flax and silk, based on their output, with gifts and garlands. Does this resemble the bonuses workers receive nowadays when businesses are profitable?

To ensure smooth operations and prevent disputes, the charges for weaving are also clearly specified in the Arthashastra.

METALS

We use all kinds of metal tools in our daily lives. A well-developed metal industry existed during Kautilya's time, and base metals like copper, steel, bronze, brass, iron and tin were used to manufacture tools, weapons and articles of household use. It appears that gold and silver jewellery studded with precious stones was as much in demand as it is today. The purity of precious metals that people buy both as ornaments and as investments has always been an issue for purchasers. It is remarkable that two thousand years ago, Kautilya thought of ways to protect the rights of consumers. The Arthashastra specifies the making charges for jewellery, which are not regulated even today. It also mentions the permissible weight loss during metal casting or forging, as well as the penalties for cheating.

SALT

If someone forgets to add salt to the curry, there will be complaints at the dinner table! Salt has always been a highly valued commodity because it adds so much flavour to food and helps to preserve it. Countries have even gone to war over it in earlier times. Salt was manufactured, and salt pans were leased to people who paid a portion of the produce to the government. Kautilya recommended that its sale price should be regulated. Different rates were to be applied to locally produced and imported edible salt, on which duties were imposed.

THE BUSINESS OF TRADE

Kautilya advised the king to promote trade as an activity essential to the economic well-being of the state and the public. Thus, trade routes were to be set up by both land and water and market towns and ports developed. The Uttarapatha and the Dakshinapatha were the famous trade routes of the time. The Uttarapatha, as its name implies, was the northern route and wound its way across the northern plains through Punjab in the west right up to Balkh in Central Asia and the port of Tamralipta in the Bay of Bengal. It was a part land and part water route since it crossed the Ganga, Yamuna, Ghaghra and Sarayu rivers. The Himalayan portion was known as the Himavatapatha and its eastern branch linked up with the Silk Route to China. The Dakshinapatha began from Shravasti in the Himalayan foothills and headed south through Varanasi, Prayag and Ujjain to Pratishthan (modern Paithan) and onward to Tamil territory. People travelled on horseback, bullock carts, chariots or even on foot. The safety of these routes was an important concern and courtiers and government officials were warned not to trouble traders. These routes were to be guarded against thieves and robbers and herds of cattle were not allowed on them in case they caused damage.

What were the goods that were transported on these routes? Horses from Central Asia and Arabia found their way to west, east and south India. Silver, lapis lazuli and other semi-precious stones came from Afghanistan, while muslin and spices travelled westwards. Gold, diamonds, rubies and pearls, sandalwood and conch shells came from the south. Silk from China, woollen blankets from Gandhara and rain-proof cloth from Nepal made its way to Indian markets. Thus, you can see that there was a thriving trade of a fascinating variety of goods.

It is said that Indian trade really took off during Mauryan times. For safety, traders travelled in caravans. Merchants known as *sarths* would invest equal amounts of capital in goods to be carried in a caravan and the leader was known as the *sarthvahak*. He supervised the movement and bore responsibility for the security of the caravan.

The National Highways project was launched after Independence. However, the Uttarapatha and Dakshinapatha are said to have been around since the time of the Mahabharata and were the base for some highways. In the sixteenth century, Sher Shah Suri made improvements to the Uttarapatha route by digging wells, building inns and planting trees, while Akbar and Jahangir improved it further. In the nineteenth century, the British made further improvements and renamed it as the Grand Trunk Road. Not just traders but military expeditions, too, found these routes useful. Buddhism also travelled to different parts of Asia via these roads.

Do you know from where the statue of the *yaksha* with a bag of money in its hand, placed in front of the Reserve Bank of India building in Delhi, originates? Created by the famous sculptor Ram Kinkar Baij, the figure of the yaksha is modeled on a statue of Manibhadra, the presiding deity of traders in Mauryan times, discovered near Mathura. Manibhadra was the son of Kubera, the god of wealth and his statues were probably placed at intervals along the Uttarapatha, since another figure was discovered near Gwalior.

Curiously, while Kautilya recognized the contribution of trade to the economy, he also proclaimed that merchants were thieves, and they should be prevented from exploiting the people!

THE MARKETING SYSTEM

The sale of goods was to be regulated, as it is in our times. The produce of the countryside could not be traded in the place of its origin. It had to be transported to the selected market in the city and could only be sold after the officially prescribed duty had been paid. In the case of commodities produced on crown or state property or received into the treasury, the officials had to give a complete sales account and hand over the proceeds along with the remaining goods and their weights and measures at the end of the day. Approved merchants were also permitted to sell crown products. Still, the prices would be fixed by the chief controller of state trading and the extra profit they made was to be the government's share. This clearly shows that Kautilya envisaged both public and private enterprise.

In contemporary times, export is considered more beneficial for the economy, but, for some reason, Kautilya gave preference to the import of goods, perhaps to make the commodities freely available to the public. Certain benefits were offered to merchants who brought in high-value products that were in demand. These could range from pearls from Sri Lanka to furs and horses from Afghanistan. Those who transported goods by caravan or water routes were exempt from taxes so that they received worthwhile returns. Foreign merchants were protected from litigation in money matters, but their local partners could be held liable.

The profit margins were fixed at five per cent for local goods and ten per cent for imported goods.

Kautilya also recommended that in the case of a glut of a particular product in the market, which led to a fall in price and losses for the producers, the chief controller of state trading should buy the commodity at a higher rate than the current market price and create a buffer stock. When the market price rose to the support level, he could bring down the official price to the suitable level.

Price control is an important issue for governments. They have to pay attention to the interests of both the producers and the consumers. Prices of commodities depend on demand and supply. When there is a bumper crop of say, wheat, prices may fall so low that farmers cannot recover the cost of production. For this reason, the Indian government sets a minimum support price (MSM) for a certain number of agricultural products. If the price falls below this, it buys the produce at the MSM from the farmers for public distribution. The Commission for Agricultural Costs and Prices (CACP) decides on this after taking various factors into account. There is also a Dual Price policy under which government procured items are sold at lower rates at fair-price shops to low-income ration card holders. However, these commodities are permitted to be sold at higher rates in the open market, too, so farmers can make a profit.

The chief controller of state trading managed the marketing of all the goods that were a state monopoly and brought considerable income to the government. He had to maintain buffer stocks, not garner too much profit and collect the transaction tax.

Kautilya also discussed the process of foreign trade. The chief controller of state trading was to examine the prospects of trade with a particular foreign country. He was to establish the cost of the goods they planned to export first, and the prices of the goods that would be imported in exchange next, then arrive at the gross margin after subtracting all the expenses. If the trade was over land using caravans, the following expenses would be considered—customs duty, road cess, tax levied at military stations, charges for escorts and ferrying the goods, daily allowances for the merchants and their helpers and the share that would be paid to the foreign king. If the trade happened by sea, there would be extra charges, like for hiring of ships and boats and the cost of provisions for the voyage.

Naturally, this trade would be viable only if profits were likely. However, Kautilya advised that even if there was no profit, it would be worthwhile to pursue it if it offered political or strategic benefits.

When sending goods in a caravan, the official in charge was to make sure that the route followed was secure. Jungle chieftains, frontier officials and the governors of the city and the countryside would be informed beforehand to guarantee a safe passage, the way we have highway police and railway police to protect travellers today.

Some scholars believe that Kautilya was the first person in recorded history to come up with the idea of customs duties. It is interesting to note that these duties were levied on all goods, whether produced in the countryside or the city or imported from other countries. Since he believed that the tax burden should not be too heavy, certain goods were tax-free, like those used to celebrate a wedding, gifts or items that would be used in rituals or to offer to the gods. In addition, the chief controller of customs could use his discretion to waive duty on products that would be of benefit to the country, like rare seeds.

Several items could not be exported. These included weapons, armours, metals, chariots, jewels and precious stones, grains and cattle. It was forbidden to import products that could cause harm to the country or had no particular use.

IMPORT AND SALE OF FOREIGN GOODS

You might wonder why a certain kind of chocolate you enjoyed during a foreign trip is not available back home. The reason is that all countries have specific foreign trade policies that govern the import of various items. Different kinds of duties are charged on goods imported as well. Customs officials also check shipments of foreign goods to ensure that rules are being followed. Interestingly, Kautilya suggested an elaborate system for regulating the import and sale of foreign goods. The frontier officer would scrutinize the caravans transporting foreign goods and categorize the merchandise according to its value. The checked packages would then be sealed with the official seal and the merchant would receive identity papers. He would collect the suitable road cess as well. After that, detailed information would be sent to the chief controller of customs.

When the caravan reached the city gates, the chief controller of customs would inspect it again and assess the merchandise, keeping the information received from the frontier officials, spies or the king in mind. Those items that were exempt from duty would be permitted to proceed. The others would be weighed, measured or counted. Several details were to be recorded—the merchant's name, place of origin, quantity of goods, the place where the merchant's identity pass was issued and where the goods were sealed.

After paying the duty, the merchant could stand near the custom house and announce the type, quantity and price of his goods. He was free to sell to anyone who agreed to the price.

Certain punishments, mostly fines, are also suggested for various offences. A merchant who added a higher margin of profit than the one prescribed or gained an unjustified profit would be fined 200 panas.

SALES THROUGH AGENTS AND RETAILERS

In contemporary times, middlemen, sales agents and retailers help farmers and manufacturers find a good market to sell their goods at a profit. Can you imagine that Kautilya envisaged this system two thousand years ago and laid down regulations to protect the rights of the producer? An agent's job was not so different from what it is today. He had to get the best price for the goods he was handling and pay the total amount realized after deducting his commission. If he did not earn a profit, he had to pay back the market value of the merchandise to the producer plus the expected profit. However, if there was an agreement between the two parties, the retailer needed to pay only the cost of the goods. If the market price of the product fell between the time that it was handed over and the sale, the value that was realized had to be paid.

Dealers who enjoyed a good reputation and had never been penalized while trading in royal goods would not be asked to pay the cost in case the material deteriorated or was lost in mischance.

Where goods were sold abroad or after a period, the expenses and losses would be deducted from the total amount payable.

In addition, separate accounts had to be maintained for different kinds of goods.

CONSUMER PROTECTION

The fact that Kautilya envisaged a state that was concerned about the welfare of its people meant that he gave much importance to the rights of the consumer. Not only artisans and craftsmen but also doctors, washermen and entertainers were to be penalized if they cheated their customers. Where workers in precious metals are concerned, the Arthashastra goes into minute detail about the methods goldsmiths and silversmiths might employ to steal from customers.

> The discerning consumer will check the Bureau of Indian Standards Hallmark for gold when buying jewellery. Surprisingly, this hallmark was introduced only in 2000 and for silver in 2005. However, it is not mandatory. Charges for working in gold and silver are still not fixed.

- The charges for working in silver and gold were fixed according to the skill required. The artisan had to complete the work within the specified time limit. In case it involved craftsmanship superior to the usual, it was not necessary to impose a deadline.

- When working on precious metals, the smiths had to make sure that the finished product they returned to the customer was of the same weight and same quality that they had received. However, some allowances were made for an acceptable loss in the making. Percentages for the shortfall are specified for gold and silver, enamelling and colouring of the metals. Weights and measures had to be purchased from the chief superintendent of weights and measures.

- The various methods with which gold and silversmiths cheated their customers are elaborated upon. To provide a false weight, they could use a balance with an arm that bent too easily or one that was hollowed and a weight put inside. They could use a split head that caused one arm to tilt more, strings not equal in length, substandard pans, or a magnet attached to pull the pan down and uneven balances. These methods would cause one pan to descend more. Thus, the weight of the item that was being sold or returned would increase, fooling the customer. A standard weight would be put into it if a customer bought or took an item.

The Ministry of Consumer Affairs, Food and Public Distribution is responsible for consumer protection in our times. The Standard of Weights and Measures Act was passed in 1976 and there are officials who are supposed to enforce the rules. The Consumer Protection Act was passed in 1986 and replaced by the Act of 2019. Many organizations exist to protect the rights of consumers and there are consumer courts to address their grievances.

- Kautilya discussed various methods to adulterate gold, including mixing it with silver and copper, using a false-bottom crucible, embedding foreign objects and adding substances like lac, vermillion or red lead. Some dishonest goldsmiths and tricksters continue to employ these techniques. He added that the purity could be tested by heating the gold and using a touchstone, scratching it to see if it was gold plated, immersing it in salt water or some chemical.

⊙ The rates for working in base metals like copper, steel, bronze, brass, lead and tin and the permitted loss in the process were also spelt out.

Rules for repairers, weavers, washermen, tailors, doctors, and entertainers were outlined. Punishments and fines were prescribed for violating rules and deceiving customers. For instance, washermen were to be fined for not using wooden boards or smooth stones for washing clothes, wearing customers' garments, selling or renting them out, as well as losing or exchanging them. Entertainers faced fines for accepting gifts to offer excessive praise, while beggars and mendicants were beaten with iron rods for moving around during the rainy season.

When you are travelling, say, by bus, train or air, the transporter is responsible for your safety and can be held liable for injuries and accidents. To protect travellers, Kautilya laid the responsibility for safe passage on the leader of a caravan. He would have to pay a fine for leaving a companion behind, whether in an inhabited place or a forest. If the abandoned person came to harm, a higher fine would be enforced. The accompanying travellers would also be penalized on the same count.

CHAPTER 4

HOW WERE FUNDS TO BE RAISED?

THE TREASURY AND SOURCES OF REVENUE

In the Arthashastra, Kautilya repeatedly emphasized the importance of having a strong financial position for the well-being of the kingdom. He said, 'Everything the kingdom does relies on money. So, a wise king should pay great attention to it.' He believed that a government's power came from the treasury. It's the treasury that provides funds for the army and allows the king to expand the kingdom's territory. That's why the treasury was given more importance than the armed forces. Kautilya advised the king to manage the army and the treasury efficiently to ensure their proper functioning.

For this very reason, the Arthashastra gives a lot of importance to the state collection of revenue. If officials caused any financial loss, they had to not only fix it but also pay a fine. This was done to show how essential it was to be particular about money matters. It's also interesting to know that there were different rules for people who paid taxes and those who didn't. If you paid taxes, you couldn't live in a village where people didn't have to pay. In some new settlements, farmers, scholars and priests got relief from paying taxes. And in some villages, instead of paying taxes, people had to work or join the army. The chief superintendent of the treasury held a position of great responsibility. His primary duty was to protect the gold, valuable items and manage the land's produce. As described earlier, there were specific directions for the location of the treasury and the warehouses within the fortified city.

Kautilya suggested several different methods of augmenting the wealth of the state. These techniques were based on common sense and were not too different from what governments pursue today. They aligned with his other theories, like ensuring all state enterprises stayed productive, maintaining tried and tested policies, preventing pilferage, keeping firm control over government employees, boosting agricultural production and promoting trade. He was conscious that natural calamities and civil unrest led to revenue losses and suggested disaster management as well.

Kautilya observed that government officials could diminish the wealth of the state by creating hindrances, misusing government property and falsifying accounts. These conditions exist today as well.

Where mishaps were concerned, Kautilya stated that a calamity that affects the fort is the most disastrous because the fort protects the treasury. Damage to the treasury has more devastating consequences than a blow to the armed forces because the treasury can supply the means to raise another army if need be.

What were the catastrophic events that could make inroads into the treasury? These could range from embezzlement by the chief officers, reduction in taxes, inefficient collection of taxes, falsification of accounts by officials in charge, to robbery of the revenue by enemies or jungle tribes en route to the treasury. To safeguard against such problems, the Arthashastra recommended constructing a large treasury on the border of the country. This was to be a secret treasure only the monarch and a few trusted people would know about.

Additionally, households were given special permission to store grains and other products which could be requisitioned by the state when needed. In other words, citizens were not allowed to hoard excessive food.

Again and again, Kautilya stressed on the need for efficient fiscal management by the king. If he paid strict attention to the collection of revenue and its expenditure, his finances would not be strained.

This theory of financial management can also apply to individuals in present times. Making a household budget, spending cautiously, saving, investing in stocks, shares and mutual funds, buying different kinds of insurance—all these are methods that provide a safety net against difficult times.

WHERE DID THE MONEY COME FROM?

A government needs funds to run public services for its citizens. Several methods of raising revenue are mentioned in the Arthashastra, mostly by way of taxes, though some rather dubious methods are listed too. The last was probably to be employed as the final resort when times were especially bad.

The four main income sources according to the Arthashastra are as follows:

- State property
- State-controlled manufacturing and entertainment
- Taxes (in cash or kind)
- Trading

In many ways, this seems quite similar to our present system. We have public sector undertakings, which are state-owned businesses, and we also have taxes on entertainment and different types of taxes on trade activities. However, taxes paid in goods instead of money are unheard of today. Back then, these taxes were called *pratikara*, and people could pay them with grain, cattle, gold, or forest products. This term also included taxes paid through labour given to the state instead of money or goods, which was known as *vishti*. In addition, villages could also pay taxes by supplying soldiers, which was called *ayudhiya*.

The system was well organized under a hierarchy of officers. The chancellor was the top official, in charge of the revenue from the countryside. The local record keepers and governors were responsible for the actual collection, but a magistrate supervised their work to see to it that it was performed efficiently, especially in the case of the Special Emergency Dues.

The state raised funds by farming its land, either directly or by leasing it out. Direct cultivation meant that the government received the net income after deducting the cost of seeds, labour etc. When the land was leased out, there were different arrangements—three-fourths or four-fifth to the state if the lessee only contributed labour, half when seeds and other inputs were provided along with labour.

Water was taxed not only when it was taken from the reservoirs built by the king but also from natural sources like ponds, lakes and rivers. The rates varied according to the methods used—manually one-fifth, by bullocks one-fourth and mechanically one-third.

Revenue from mines was another important source of income for the state. This included all kinds of metals and precious stones. Several officials were appointed to supervise the mining, processing and trade of these. They were the chief controller of mining and metallurgy, the chief superintendent of mines, the chief superintendent of metals, the chief master of the mint, the chief coin examiner and the chief salt commissioner. Mines could be directly under the state's control or leased out. The state retained the ones that were easier to work on without too much cost and leased out those where the extraction was more difficult. The working of metals was a state enterprise and their trade was centralized too. Kautilya accords high value to the produce of mines. Not only could they bring in an income through sales to the people, but also the metals could be used to manufacture all kinds of goods and implements, including weapons for the army. The revenue raised from mines was thus through the sale of gems minus the expenditure on labour, the sale of metals minus the cost of mining and processing, and similarly, the sale of alloys minus the manufacturing input.

The Crown also owned herds of cattle, which could be managed directly or contracted out. In the first instance, the sale of ghee and all by-products came directly to the king, while the contractor had to pay a certain amount for each animal along with a percentage of the by-products. The animal by-products included hair, skins, bladders, bile, tendons, teeth, hooves and horns, as well as wool from sheep and goats.

In addition, fish, ducks and green vegetables cultivated near reservoirs also belonged to the king since the land was his property.

Timber and other products from forests were owned by the state, as were the products manufactured from these. Does this sound like most of the wealth of the country belonged to the king?

> Today too, forests are the property of the government in India and managed by the Forest Department. They are classified as reserved, protected and unclassed forests. Reserved forests make up fifty per cent of our forest area. They are classified as such for forest and wildlife conservation. Protected forests make up one-third and are so classified to maintain forest cover. Unclassed forests can be government-owned, privately owned or managed by local communities.

The kind of industry we have today did not exist then. Textiles were produced, as earlier mentioned, and these also brought an income to the state.

Salt pans were leased out, and revenue was derived from the rent as earlier mentioned. It could be a percentage of the salt produced, which was purchased by the public. Duty was also charged on imported salt.

Alcoholic beverages were also manufactured by the state to be sold to the public in state-controlled bars. These were under the charge of the chief controller of alcoholic beverages. Those that were privately brewed paid a five per cent monopoly tax.

There was even an official called the chief controller of entertainers who collected taxes from prostitutes, courtesans and other entertainers. He had to keep detailed accounts of the money he received and furnish one-sixth of his income or five panas per show, in the case of foreign entertainers.

Gambling and betting were permitted and an official titled the chief controller of gambling would levy a charge of five per cent on winnings.

Custom duties were charged on goods entering and leaving the city, which would be collected at the gates. Octroi and a few other kinds of toll taxes were also there. A tax called *gudma* was also charged at military stations and pickets.

Every transaction attracted a tax, which could be described as a sales tax, revenue surcharge, or a discount on government payments. This was known as *vyaji*.

Butchers had to pay taxes to the chief protector of animals and the controller of animal slaughter. Certain animals were protected from slaughter, especially those in sanctuaries. This shows us that the idea of animal sanctuaries is not a modern one.

Road cess was collected by ferrymen at the borders and charged on head loads, small animals, cattle and cartloads.

Taxes were levied for ferry services or protection by the army when required. There was a stamping fee for weights and measures, passport fees, port dues, land survey charges. When new coins were issued, there was a coining fee and a certain testing fee for coins deposited in the treasury.

Different kinds of fines were imposed, which brought in a marginal income but were probably imposed in the interest of maintaining law and order and preventing corruption among officials.

Prisoners could redeem themselves by paying fines or someone else could pay on their behalf. Curiously, a charge was levied for reclaiming lost property.

The Crown was at an advantage in almost every kind of transaction. If a property dispute could not be settled, the king would acquire it. If a man died without leaving an heir, his property would go to the king too, but a deduction could be made for funeral expenses and for the upkeep of the widow.

Apart from all these sources, foreign tribute was added to the king's coffers along with treaty payments.

Kautilya suggested enforcing special levies and taxes if a king was strapped for cash. Some of these sound strange and unethical.

The chancellor could request donations from the citizens using the excuse of a state project when there was a shortfall of revenue. To motivate people to donate, secret agents would pretend to gift large amounts and then be held up as examples.

Kautilya also suggested that the king could request the wealthy to donate gold. He could offer honours in return, for example, certain kinds of umbrellas, headgear or decorations.

Another dubious method was to grab the property and wealth of temples using vague excuses. This is reminiscent of Henry VIII of England seizing the property of monasteries to fill up his exchequer when he broke away from the church of Rome.

It seems that if the king was running short of finances, any trick could be employed!

BUDGET, ACCOUNTS AND AUDIT

The presentation of the budget by the finance minister of our country is a major event today. It's fascinating to discover that Kautilya was conscious of its importance and had made the chancellor responsible for preparing the annual budget of the kingdom.

The chancellor was to make an estimate of the prospective revenue by listing what was expected from each region and field of activity under various heads of account and then add it up to make the grand total.

Then he was to gauge the actual revenue by adding the amounts paid into the treasury during the current year and any amounts that were pending from the year before. He would then subtract the expenditure—on the king, rations paid out, tax exemptions and permitted deferments of payment.

Revenue that was yet to be paid was calculated by listing projects that would yield an income when complete, fines and penalties that had not been paid, dues that were pending or being deliberately withheld and advances taken by officials that had not been reimbursed. Minor amounts were not to be taken into consideration.

The actual income was categorized into three main areas:

i) Current income: This referred to the revenues that were owed or paid within the same year.

ii) Transferred income: This category encompassed revenue originating from unpaid dues of the previous year, as well as income generated by one department and transferred to another.

iii) Miscellaneous revenue: This included three types of income sources. Firstly, it involved the retrieval of unpaid debts and previously abandoned dues. Secondly, it comprised fines paid by officials, income from surcharges and unexpected earnings, compensation for loss and damage, as well as ownerless property that reverted to the state and treasure trove. Lastly, it accounted for savings resulting from the demobilization of a portion of the army and profits from sales of commodities by the state. Actual expenditure would be listed under the headings of budgeted daily expenses, unbudgeted daily expenses and predicted fortnightly, monthly and annual expenses. The revenue would be assessed by subtracting expenditure from earnings while keeping the real figures and the overdue amounts in mind.

Kautilya gave detailed instructions for keeping accounts. The account books were to be maintained according to the prescribed format and written clearly without corrections. They had to be submitted at the end of the month, or else the official would be penalized. Where specific transactions were concerned, a delay of five days for paying into the treasury was excusable if the amount was small. If remittance of the revenue was not done within five days, an extensive audit would be done after the payment had been made to examine the reasons. Secret agents came into the picture here too.

The duties of the account officers have also been elaborated upon. They were to be punctual in attending the audit and bring their account books along with the sum to be deposited in the treasury. When called upon by the auditor, they were to be fully prepared and answer him truthfully. It was forbidden to attempt adding an entry that had been missed by pretending it was an unintentional omission. If they failed to follow these rules they would be penalized.

In the event of an irregularity, like showing a smaller amount than what was actually due, the official would have to pay a fine. However, if the amount due to the treasury was less than what the official had noted, the difference would be paid to him.

The auditors were also exhorted to perform their duties efficiently or face punishment. The punishments for different offences like sloppy entries, overwriting or indecipherable entries are prescribed. Losing account books, destroying them, even by accident, delays in submission, not being punctual about attending the audit, neglecting to bring account books or revenue, falsifying accounts, all invited fines ranging from twelve to 200 panas or percentages of the loss to the state.

In this way, Kautilya advised strict control on the officials to avoid leakage of revenue.

CHAPTER 5

BABUDOM ACCORDING TO KAUTILYA

THE RULES OF THE CIVIL SERVICE

The civil service that handles administration in our country today is a colonial legacy from the time of British rule. Interestingly, the one Kautilya planned in the Arthashastra is, in many ways, not too different from it.

Kautilya extensively outlined the administrative structure of an ideal state in book two of the Arthashastra, which happens to be the longest book within the work. With a total of thirty-six chapters, it comprises approximately a quarter of the entire work. These chapters explicitly specify the responsibilities assigned to various government departments. The book lists around thirty-four different department heads, covering almost every aspect of government activity. These officials, referred to as *adhyakshas*, do not appear to possess equal status, indicating the existence of a hierarchical system, much like the one we observe in present times.

The officers did not receive the same salary, nor did all the departments possess equal importance. An official who did not perform well was to be transferred to a lower-level department. The administrative hierarchy and the organization of administrative officers are also described.

HOW WERE CIVIL SERVANTS RECRUITED?

Today, thousands of young women and men sit for the much sought-after Union Public Service Commission or civil service examinations. However, this system did not exist in those distant times in our country, though an examination for bureaucrats was introduced in ancient China in 206 BCE. The process of appointment of civil servants was interesting because here too, secret agents played an important role, which showed the dependence of the Kautilyan state on intelligence gathering. Disguised as ascetics, spies were to act as talent scouts, seeking out intelligent, dynamic and articulate men for different posts. Afterwards, their names were confidentially suggested to the minister as suitable candidates.

Those who possessed the required abilities would be appointed as heads of departments. Each department functioned with a network of accountants, clerks, coin examiners, storekeepers and military advisers. Assistants to the military supervisors would keep an eye on the lower-grade officials, like accountants and clerks.

THE DEPARTMENTS OF THE GOVERNMENT

The treasury department being extremely important, two officers were in charge—the chief superintendent of the treasury and the chief superintendent of the warehouses. Even today, the gold reserve of a country, held by its central bank in the form of bullion, is considered an indispensable financial asset. In Kautilya's time, gems, jewellery, precious metals and other valuable products were part of the treasury. The governor of the Reserve Bank of India is always a highly qualified economist. Similarly, the treasury superintendent was expected to be knowledgeable about the value of the treasury holding, manage finances and maintain records meticulously.

It is apparent that it was a society that enjoyed many objects of luxury, considering that the qualities of many different gems are written about in the Arthashastra, along with the places they could be sourced from. Diamonds and pearls, rubies, beryls, sapphires are mentioned along with semi-precious stones and coral. Perfumery items like sandalwood, aloe, incense, camphor and calica are also described. Manufactured jewellery, woollen cloth and blankets along with fabrics like silk and cotton are some of the other articles of use discussed.

The chief superintendent of warehouses supervised the granaries and warehouses where all kinds of products were stored. These were somewhat like the warehouses of the Food Corporation of India, which was formed to ensure food security for the citizens of our country.

The Arthashastra mentions departments of government as extensive as those we have today—ranging from agriculture, trade and industry to fields like entertainment. The duties of the officials manning these departments are listed in great detail. All the chief officials had a group of subordinates working under them. To prevent misuse of power and corruption, the heads of departments were to be transferred frequently.

If you wish to travel to a different country, you cannot enter it without a passport, which is a proof of your identity. Even within our own country, we need identity proof to board a train or flight. We may think that such identity cards and passports are a modern phenomenon. However, even in those times, Kautilya advised the appointment of movement-control officials to keep an eye on internal and external travel by its citizens. A chief passport officer was to give out passes stamped with the official seal, and there was a charge for them. These would be checked by frontier guards and other officials, including the chief controller of pasture lands.

Temples and holy places were to be supervised by the government too.

So, you can see that an extensive bureaucratic network covering all the spheres of state activity is envisioned in the Arthashastra.

THE KING'S WATCHFUL EYE

What happens when your teacher leaves the classroom for some reason? Does everyone sit quietly attending to their classwork? Some students will but others might get up to all kinds of mischief. However, the moment the teacher returns, a hush falls over the classroom.

Keeping this aspect of human nature in mind, Kautilya emphasized that the head of a government needs to be well informed and must exercise strict control to guarantee its effective functioning. He advised the king to be vigilant and inspect the work of the heads of departments daily. The king was to keep himself updated about the officer in charge of a particular project, the kind of work it was, the place it was being executed at and the time frame for its completion, as well as the costs and expected profit.

Any project undertaken was to receive proper authorization unless it was an emergency situation. Officers are exhorted to cooperate with each other and not indulge in petty bickering because it would affect the project adversely. Neither were they to conspire to cheat the king by embezzling revenue. Here again, the carrot-and-stick method was suggested—inefficient officers would be fined double their wages as well as their actual expenses and efficient ones would be rewarded with promotions and incentives.

The heads of departments would have to give accurate reports to the king about the work performed and let him know in detail about the revenue earned as well as the expenses incurred.

Kautilya listed three pitfalls that could lead to a deficiency in collecting revenue. The first was a loss because of negligence, the second was being overly enthusiastic and collecting an excessive amount, thus alienating the public, and the third was being lax in maintaining a balance between income and expenses.

The king could not be everywhere at the same time, so he had to rely on his intelligence network for information. Kautilya didn't believe that an official who was not gathering enough revenue and who was a big spender was necessarily corrupt. Only the secret agents watching him could provide the correct picture.

The king was supposed to keep an eye on the officers who squandered their inheritance, as well as those who blew up their salary as soon as they received it, or those who were so miserly that they hoarded their cash while their families lived in want. This shows that he believed that personal habits of money management revealed whether the official was right for his job.

An official whose actions resulted in a loss of income to the state was to be dismissed, but if he had dependents, his property should not be confiscated. If an official who was stingy by nature was amassing the king's revenue for his own use by storing it in his own house or using it to trade with foreigners, secret agents were to ferret out all the details of this embezzlement. When his guilt was established, he was to be charged with being in the pay of the enemy by producing a forged letter as evidence. The penalty suggested seems rather extreme. Execution.

Kautilya makes other suggestions about keeping different officials in line and seeing to it that they discharged their duties sincerely. If an inspector was careless and it resulted in a loss to the exchequer, this amount would be recovered from his colleagues, those who stood surety for him, subordinates, sons, brothers, wives, daughters, or servants.

The different reasons for a shortfall in revenue have been mentioned. One is insufficient knowledge of the task to be performed, rules, regulations and customs. Another is the official's laziness or him neglecting his work to have a good time. It could also be timidity because the official did not want to displease people and feared the repercussions of being strict or feared criminal-minded people. Corruption is also mentioned as a cause of loss of revenue, especially if the official was inclined to favour his associates. It was also possible that an official might antagonize the public, from whom he had to collect taxes, because of his bad temper and violent nature. An official who was conceited because he was knowledgeable or overconfident because he was backed by influential people could also cause a loss. The last reason mentioned is greed which prompts an official to falsify weights and measures and make incorrect assessments and calculations.

Kautilya suggested that the punishment given should be in proportion to the seriousness of the crime and each situation should be assessed in its proper context rather than taking a blanket approach. These punishments consisted of fines for different kinds of lapses or dismissal from service, the most severe being execution, as earlier mentioned.

CORRUPTION AMONG OFFICIALS

The issue of corruption among officials and its effect on the country's progress is often hotly discussed today. Kautilya was very conscious of this problem. He even said: 'Just as it is impossible to know when a fish moving in water is drinking it, so it is impossible to find out where a government servant in charge of undertakings is misappropriating money.'

Misappropriation of government funds was taken as a serious crime and various punishments were suggested for it. Kautilya mentioned forty ways of stealing, ranging from embezzling government funds to other kinds of cheating. In these cases, an investigation would be made, and all the officials concerned would be questioned separately. Those who gave false answers would be penalized as severely as the officer who had committed the crime. Members of the public who had suffered because of this offence could respond to the accusations made. They would be compensated for any loss caused to them.

If there were several accusations of cheating against an officer and he refused to admit to any of them, he would be held accountable for all of them if he was proven guilty even on one count. In the case of a fraud involving a large sum of money, if the entire offence could not be proved, the accused would be punished for the portion that could.

Informers would be rewarded even if they had participated in the crime. The informer was also to receive protection from the accused. Much like we have 'safe houses' for witnesses today, the informer would either be housed safely at a secret location or his identity kept confidential by naming someone else as the informer. However, if the offence could not be proved, the informer would either be fined or have some physical punishment meted out to him. If an informer went back on his testimony and collaborated with the accused, he would be condemned to execution.

Several punishments for guilty civil servants are listed. Stealing from the king was considered the most heinous crime. It invited the death penalty, especially if the theft was of valuable articles like gems. Death by torture is also suggested. Other crimes like stealing public property, false documentation, wrongful confinement and administrative lapses invited fines of different amounts. Public humiliation was another form of punishment and included smearing with cow dung in public, parading with a belt of broken pots and shaving off the head. Incidentally, some of these punishments are still used by people in our country to shame offenders!

THE DUTIES OF CITIZENS

We expect the government to manage its affairs well so as to provide us with a decent quality of life. But to accomplish it, as citizens we have certain duties too. The Arthashastra discusses the duties of citizens in both rural and urban areas. Village headmen had certain responsibilities, like making boundaries around the village, protecting the fields and pastures, collecting revenue and enforcing laws. The inhabitants of the village had to follow a prescribed code of conduct. Villages were organized in a social hierarchy where Brahmins occupied the highest position and had certain privileges. Importance was given to community work, and everyone was expected to pitch in to contribute both labour and cash, whether for a festival, entertainment or the agricultural activities of the village. Failure to do so invited a fine. Grazing charges were levied, and penalties were imposed if cattle damaged other people's crops. These fines went to the village, not the state.

As for the inhabitants of cities, certain responsibilities have been detailed too. These relate to fire prevention, hygiene, construction activities, causing injury to others and damage to public and private property. Believe it or not, a traffic code has been listed. For example, a cart was not allowed to move without a driver, and a minor driver had to be accompanied by an adult. So it seems that our current rules for learner drivers have a long history! If a driver injured another person because of careless driving, he would be punished. Sounds familiar?

Kautilya displays much consideration for the privacy of citizens. The public was warned against prying into their neighbours' affairs. However, it was their duty to come to the aid of a neighbour in distress. Citizens had to contribute their share in the construction of common facilities and be careful not to damage them. Plants and trees in city parks, sanctuaries, holy places and cremation grounds were not to be vandalized, especially those that bore fruit or flowers and provided shade.

There were also regulations for constructing houses. Since the thatched-roof houses were extremely vulnerable, particular attention was given to fire prevention. In summer, the citizens were not allowed to light fires in the first and second quarters of the day. If it was essential, they could cook outside the house. This practice of having cooking fires outside persists in some areas to this day. Every household had to contribute five water pots, a big jar, a trough, a ladder, an axe for chopping down beams and pillars, a winnowing basket to fan away flames, a hook to pull away burning parts, and a hooked rake to pull down burning thatch. When a house caught fire, whoever was in the vicinity had to come forward to help douse it.

These days, there is much talk of the Swachh Bharat Abhiyan. This concern for public hygiene has, however, existed since ancient times. The Arthashastra warned citizens not to throw dirt in the streets or let mud and water collect. The royal highways were to be kept especially clean. People were forbidden from passing urine and stools near holy places, water reservoirs, temples or royal property and no one was permitted to throw dead bodies of animals or human beings inside the city. There was a prescribed route for transporting corpses out of the city and specific places were designated for cremation and burial.

The Swachh Bharat Abhiyan, or Clean India Mission, was launched in 2014. As its name suggests, its objective is to improve sanitation in our country. Toilets have been constructed to end the practice of defecation in open places, encourage waste management, end manual scavenging and promote public hygiene. It is based on earlier sanitation missions which were launched from time to time.

CHAPTER 6

TOWARDS JUSTICE AND AN ORDERLY SOCIETY

In William Golding's classic young adult book *Lord of the Flies*, a group of schoolboys are marooned on an island. Removed from civilized society and the restraint of rules, little by little the boys abandon their moral code and descend into savagery. The novel demonstrates without a system that enforces discipline, how easily human beings can surrender to uncontrolled violent impulses.

Kautilya has touched upon almost every aspect of governance in the ideal state he projects in the Arthashastra. The justice system naturally finds a place here—in fact, this is considered the first detailed legal code expounded in India. Since the king held all authority, to emphasize the importance of ensuring that the citizens of a country receive fair treatment, he comments, 'The king who observes his duty of protecting his people justly and according to law will go to heaven, whereas one who does not protect them or inflicts unjust punishment will not.'

This idea is expressed in the Mahabharata, too, while the concept of the ideal king, one who is always just, is found in many of our traditional stories like those about King Vikramaditya.

The king, being all-in-all, had the responsibility of upholding the rules of ethical conduct and could frame laws to enforce this code, especially when people disregarded the traditional codes of decent behaviour.

According to Kautilya, it was the government's responsibility to maintain the social order as well as prevent and punish criminal activity. To this end, he defined systems of both civil and criminal law. Family law, the law of contracts and the law of labour were included under civil law. The customary law of the people of a particular region or group was also to be considered. Apart from this, the king could frame laws in the form of edicts so that the information became public knowledge.

In the Arthashastra, the judge is described as *dharmastha* or the upholder of dharma. This reveals that dharma was deemed the source of all law. Kautilya believed that if every citizen followed his *swadharma* or personal code, according to his varna and ashram and the king maintained his raj dharma, the social order would be preserved as desired.

The basic idea behind the rule of law is the smooth functioning of society to guarantee the welfare of a country's citizens by treating all of them as equals under the law of the land. In modern democracies, laws are framed by the elected representatives of the people rather than a monarch. A written constitution for the country ensures it by binding the government to certain principles so that the head of state and others in power cannot act in an arbitrary manner. These laws need to be enforced impartially to make them effective. That is why a judicial system exists so the common man can appeal against injustice. A judiciary that is independent from other branches of government is considered essential to maintain the rule of law so that each citizen can receive fair treatment.

Our modern–day laws are also based on moral concepts like honesty in our dealings, abjuring violence, respecting the rights of other citizens, regulating social behaviour and protecting the weaker sections of society, among others. The main difference is that in Kautilya's time, society was not as egalitarian as we try to make it today, and certain classes and castes received preferential treatment. So, it cannot be said that each citizen was equal under the law. Punishments may have had the same objective, but they were much harsher and many seem barbaric by modern standards.

Kautilya covers crimes like assault, homicide, rape and corruption that are included in the Indian Penal Code. More remarkably, he has mentioned penalties for cruelty against animals, wildlife protection and deforestation, which have been added to many penal codes in recent times. The Pocso Act was passed only in 2012 in India. But in that distant era, Kautilya had advocated severe punishments for sexual abuse of children.

The judges or *dharmasthas* were to rule on cases that concerned transactions between two parties—commercial transactions, marriage, inheritance, property, debts etc. These crimes were usually punished with fines.

Magistrates or *pradestris* are also mentioned as judicial officers in the Arthashastra. They dealt with crimes against society like fraud, theft, corruption and murder. The punishments were naturally more severe and included torture, mutilation and execution apart from fines. Magistrates had executive duties as well as judicial ones. Apart from investigating crimes, they helped revenue officials collect taxes and dues. They were responsible for inspecting the work of the record keepers and provincial governors and had to make sure that taxes were being duly collected.

These two classes of officers served under the chancellor. Their appointments were dependent on their qualifications, which were expected to be of the same level as those of a minister. There would be benches of three judges or three magistrates in each jurisdiction.

Judgments had to be based on four principles of justice. These were:

⊙ Dharma, based on truth
⊙ Evidence, which came from witnesses
⊙ Custom, which meant the traditions of that particular group of people. These were mostly regarding religious observances, inheritance or the marriage customs of a particular community.
⊙ Royal edicts, these were the laws made by the ruling monarch, which were proclaimed publicly. Some of Ashoka's rock edicts ban animal slaughter and advocate tolerance towards all religions.

When custom and the Dharmashastra were not in agreement in a case, or there was a conflict between the evidence and the Shastras, dharma had the final say. In the event that the Shastras and the written law derived from dharma had opposing views, the written law was given precedence. This aligns with modern interpretations where statutory law takes precedence over customary law.

Customary or community law has played an essential role in delivering justice and regulating human activity since ancient times. The Constitution of India recognizes customary law under Article 13, and this recognition has been prevalent even during colonial times. For instance, the Hindu Marriage Act and the Hindu Succession Act are built upon customary practices. However, if there is a conflict between customary law and statutory law, the former will not be upheld.

A bench of three judges was to hold court at frontier posts, sub-district headquarters and provincial headquarters. They were expected to be knowledgeable in the finer aspects of dharma. Additionally, they were advised to maintain objectivity and fairness in their judgments to earn the people's confidence and respect.

A particular code of behaviour was prescribed for these officials.

A judge was not to threaten, intimidate, drive away, or prevent a litigant from speaking up. He could not abuse anyone appearing before him, neglect to ask relevant questions or put forward immaterial questions. He was not to ignore replies applicable to his questions. In addition, he could not coach the litigant in answering questions or remind him facts. It was his duty to pay attention and ask for

appropriate evidence while not inviting unrelated testimony. A case could not be decided without proper evidence or dismissed without a valid reason. He could not drive litigants to abandon a case by exhausting them with delays. Neither could he misrepresent a statement made in a particular context, instruct witnesses or pass judgement on a case that had already been concluded. The judge who violated these rules could be penalized and if the offence was repeated, he would be fined double the amount in question and removed from office.

The judges' clerks had to record the statements made in court accurately and not make any additions. Even if the evidence was ambiguous, they had to record it just the way it was stated. They were not permitted to distort or change the evidence.

When the judges and magistrates passed sentences, they were expected to have a balanced approach while awarding punishment. They were not at liberty to impose fines lower or higher than the prescribed ones. Their duty was to make sure that justice was done where claims were concerned. The Arthashastra recommends punishments for judges and magistrates who do not perform their duties as instructed.

The details of legal procedure and the entire process of filing a suit, recording statements, countersuits and rejoinders are clearly described in the Arthashastra. The law of evidence is also set forth in detail. Time was to be allotted to the accused party to prepare a defence. Witnesses were to take an oath before a Brahmin, a water jar or a fire. Those who misrepresented the truth were to be fined twenty-four panas, twelve if they refused to testify.

Apart from fines, there were punishments for delaying testimony, perjury, not filing a suit at the required time and claiming more than the justified amount. Absconders were severely penalized.

LAWS OF INHERITANCE AND WOMEN'S RIGHTS

Kautilya recognized that many aspects of private and public existence were interlinked and the smooth functioning of daily life ultimately contributed to the prosperity of a kingdom. Since most of his policies were aimed at the general welfare of the public, along with listing the laws of inheritance and marriage, he discussed women's rights in detail. This is an interesting aspect of the Arthashastra, considering that even today, laws regarding women's rights to education, employment and inheritance continue to be a matter of public debate.

We receive a vivid picture of the social setup through these definitions, which give us an idea of how society and the legal system have evolved in our country over the ages. By Mauryan times, marriage between people from different varnas and castes had apparently become acceptable. There was no deep-rooted prejudice against widow remarriage, like at a later period in history. Women were accorded a particular status in society—they had a certain amount of freedom and could own property, but were mostly subject to the men in their lives.

Kautilya has followed the traditional Hindu practice as set forth in the Dharmashastras when specifying the laws of inheritance. When a man died, his male children would inherit his property because it was assumed that the sons would perform the funeral rites and annual ceremonies for their father and other ancestors. The eldest son was entitled to the largest share. It was his responsibility to support his younger brothers and sisters, along with his father's other wives, since polygamy existed at the time. Unmarried sons were to receive sums of money equal to the amount that was spent on the weddings of their other brothers, and provisions had to be made for the marriages of unmarried daughters. Daughters did not receive a share in their father's property. Still, they could inherit their mother's jewellery and bronze household utensils after her death. However, if there were no sons, the daughters could inherit everything. This partition of property had to be done in front of witnesses and each share had to be publicly announced. If there were no heirs, the property would revert to the king, excluding the sums of money needed for the maintenance of the widow and performing the funeral rites.

The Arthashastra mentions eight different forms of marriage and the rituals and rules governing them. Arranged marriages have been the norm in our country over the ages, though the custom of swayamvara existed in royal families in earlier times. According to Kautilya, however, a girl had the liberty to choose her own husband if her father failed to arrange her marriage when she reached a suitable age. Dowry was given in the form of jewellery and other gifts at the time of marriage. This was known as *streedhana* and meant for the woman's personal use.

During British Rule, Indian women lost control over their dowry or streedhana when Governor-General Lord Cornwallis enacted his Permanent Settlement in 1793. This law introduced private ownership of land and denied property rights to women. Consequently, after marriage, the dowry given by a girl's parents became the property of her husband. This transformation turned dowry into a form of ransom extracted from the bride's parents, leading to criminal practices such as female infanticide.

A woman was also entitled to a sum of money for her support from her husband along with jewellery.

When a man went off on a long journey without providing for his family, the wife was entitled to use her endowment to support her sons and daughters-in-law. The husband had the right to spend his wife's money on religious activities and in emergencies such as disease or famine.

Interestingly, if a wife passed away before her husband, her children had priority over her husband in inheritance. Sons and daughters would receive shares of equal value. In case she had no sons, her daughters would divide it amongst themselves equally. The husband could only inherit if she was childless.

Apparently, widow remarriage was acceptable in those days. However, a widow who did not intend to get remarried would inherit whatever endowment her husband had settled on her, along with her jewellery, the remnants of her dowry and anything else that her husband had given her in his lifetime. This property would be inherited by her sons eventually. If a widow decided to remarry, she could not claim any of the property left by her deceased husband. A woman was also permitted to remarry if her husband left her without providing for her after a particular period had lapsed.

Kautilya further explores other possible situations, like a widow with sons remarrying. In such an event, her property would pass on to her sons.

Polygamy was permissible, but there were certain conditions. A man was to allow each wife control over her dowry and property and provide for all their maintenance. Those who did not have any dowry or property of their own would receive proper maintenance, as well as some compensation. The man was expected to treat all his wives equally.

A wife had the option of leaving her husband if he was a person of questionable character or if he left home for a long time to travel in foreign lands. Also, if he betrayed the king or threatened her life. Husband and wife were supposed to maintain a courteous relationship and abusive behaviour could be punished. A husband could not stop his wife from visiting her family on occasions like death, illness, or childbirth.

There were also provisions for divorce, which reflect Kautilya's practical approach to relationship issues and seem quite modern. In the case of a separation, the husband was to pay maintenance according to his income, while the wife's financial status was also considered.

Women were forbidden to travel unescorted by their families. Nuns and entertainers, however, were not restricted. This seems like a practical approach since many of these women worked as spies!

OF LOANS AND PLEDGES

Shakespeare might have proclaimed, 'Neither a borrower nor a lender be', but human needs make it next to impossible to rule out borrowing and lending of money. People take out loans for specific purposes, like buying a house or when they run short of money for their needs. They may approach banks, financial institutions or private moneylenders. There may be extensive paperwork for the transaction or just an 'IOU', an informal document acknowledging a loan. Defaulting on a loan, however, can lead to all kinds of problems for both the borrower and the lender.

Kautilya well understood the need to frame laws concerning loans, deposits, pledges and mortgages to maintain a harmonious polity. Since there was limited scope for paperwork at that time, he advised that such transactions should be executed in the presence of witnesses and the terms regarding time, place, quality and quantity made crystal clear.

He did not regard loans between family members like husband and wife, father and son, and brothers in a joint family as legally recoverable. A wife could not be held liable for her husband's debts if she had not given her assent, except in the case of farmers' and herdsmen's families. A husband was bound to pay his wife's debts if he had left without providing for her.

The interest on the loan of a debtor who was engaged in lengthy rituals, ill or studying with a teacher, a minor or bankrupt was not to be increased. If the creditor had not tried to recover his loan for ten years, he could not claim it. An exception was made for minors, the ill, the aged, those on long journeys and those suffering due to some disaster or unrest in the kingdom.

Any surety given was for a specific transaction and could not be applied to other matters.

What exactly is a surety? A surety is a guarantee that a person taking a loan will repay it. An individual or organization can undertake to provide this surety on behalf of a borrower, which means that they guarantee the repayment of the loan. Banks ask for guarantors while giving loans. If the borrower defaults, the guarantor must pay. It is interesting to think that Kautilya covered so many similar aspects of loans in the Arthashastra.

If a man died in debt, his sons, other heirs, co-signatories and those who stood as guarantors were bound to meet his obligations, unless the terms were for a particular period or place.

When any property, including animals and slaves, was entrusted for safekeeping to another person, he could not be prosecuted if he failed to return it in case of any calamity like fire, looting or war. On the other hand, if this deposit was used for personal gain, the depositor would have to be compensated. It could not be sold, misused, substituted or lost.

The rate of interest was to be fixed at the time of giving a loan and could not be changed.

Similarly, laws regarding pledges, transport and delivery orders, borrowing and hiring find their place in the Arthashastra. Even work entrusted to artisans and craftsmen is regulated, which means that consumer protection is given importance. All the fines and punishments for flouting these rules are listed as well.

The Arthashastra has not neglected laws concerning property. Proof of ownership can be defined by continuity of possession if any other kind is not available. Similarly, the principle of adverse possession is recognized in the case of property unclaimed for ten years or a building in which the owner had not lived for twenty years. The Arthashastra states that disputes can be resolved based on the neighbours' testimony. It is fascinating to note that this principle of adverse possession still remains legal in our country. A tenant or any other person who had been occupying a property uninterrupted for twelve years can claim adverse possession and become its owner.

Slavery and bonded labour existed at that time and Kautilya also laid down regulations for their humane treatment, particularly of women and children. They could be redeemed without opposition from their employer and small children could not be forced to work. Similarly, labourers were to be paid fair wages according to the task they were engaged for. Payment was to be made for extra work, much like overtime is compensated in our times. Significantly, the rights of both employees and employers are listed in detail.

Criminal investigations are also extensively covered. The methods of investigating crimes ranging from burglary to violent robbery, dishonesty by artisans and murder are all described. It may sound astonishing, but ways to conduct a post-mortem examination to establish unnatural death are mentioned, like smearing oil on the body to highlight injuries and identifying cases of strangulation or poisoning. Motive was to be established while questioning suspects and witnesses.

Laws regarding the punishment of crime, defamation, assault, theft and robbery have all been listed. Some seem extreme from our point of view, like death penalty for certain kinds of theft or cutting off noses and ears.

Isn't it amazing that the legal system Kautilya envisaged in ancient India covers most of the offences encountered in contemporary times? It shows how wide-ranging was the depth and breadth of thought that went into the compilation of the Arthashastra.

CHAPTER 7

ABOUT SPIES AND SECRET AGENTS

What profession do you think a *gudapurusha*, *samastha*, *kapatika*, *udasthitha*, *sattri*, *tikshna* or *parivrajika* followed? These are all categories of spies mentioned in the Arthashastra.

WHY DOES A GOVERNMENT NEED SPIES?

Throughout history and even today, the cloak-and-dagger department occupies an important position in the challenging business of governing a country.

A well-organized intelligence network has always been pivotal for ensuring the security and prosperity of any nation. The Arthashastra recognizes these individuals who dwell in the shadows, adopting disguises and operating under fake identities, often braving grave risks, as indispensable for the effective governance of a country. The treatise goes into extensive detail on the methods of selecting and setting up a network of spies and secret agents, their categories, their training and their operations. It considers this the next important task a ruler must attend to after he has appointed his prime minister and the council of ministers.

WHAT WAS KAUTILYA'S INTELLIGENCE NETWORK LIKE?

According to Kautilya, this had to be an elaborate organization with various categories of spies. A pyramidal structure was recommended. There would be spies reporting only to the ruler, who could be either a man or a woman. This category of spies was described as *guda* or concealed. Some agents were to be stationed permanently in one place, undercover and were called *samastha* or established. Others, known as *sattris*, were travelling agents who were sent on special assignments. Both categories adopted some other profession as a cover for their clandestine activities. The established head agents would gather the secret information from the others—the *kapatikas* or intelligence officers—and put it together and pass it on to the authorities, using a code. They were all permanent employees of the government and were paid salaries. The established agents would receive about 1000 panas—the currency of the time—per year, while the roaming agents received 500. However, there were also agents who were hired on a consignment basis and paid for each job they executed, usually about 250 panas.

These were political agents, but the head of the revenue department had his own network of spies who kept a lookout for people who were not paying their taxes and also for suspicious strangers and lawbreakers.

We have a number of agencies that gather different kinds of intelligence in India today. The Central Bureau of Investigation (CBI) is the principal police agency investigating criminal matters within the country. The Research and Analysis Wing (RAW) deals with intelligence matters concerning our hostile neighbours like Pakistan and China. The Intelligence Bureau (IB) monitors different aspects of governance as well as counter-terrorism. There is also the National Investigative Agency, which investigates many matters, including terrorism, the Defence Intelligence Agency and the Narcotics Control Bureau, among others.

Often, we come across situations in books and movies where a man or woman's family members are astonished to discover that they are actually spies. This kind of cover—of an ordinary householder—was suggested and probably common in ancient India too, since a family man does not stand out as different or suspicious. The head of intelligence in a region or city could well be a merchant or a professional man who juggled two jobs—one public, the other secret. He could even be an *udastitha*, a monk residing in a monastery, using the cover of his supposedly blameless religious identity. He could also adopt the disguise of an ascetic who has renounced the world.

Secret agents like James Bond, who has a 'license to kill' appear to be daring characters in the fictional world of today. Their counterparts are discussed in the Arthashastra as well. They were assassins who were well-trained in the use of weapons and poisons. They were called *tikshna* or those who used sharp practices. The poisoners, who had special knowledge of toxic substances, were known as *rasadas*. They were employed to act against enemy rulers or others perceived as a threat to the head of state. Among them, you would find both men and women, and they were among the category of spies who had to travel wherever their jobs took them.

As in contemporary times, double agents were also employed. These could be spies working for an enemy, who would be coerced to inform against the original employer, perhaps by holding their families hostage. The possibility that the ruler's agents might be working for others was also to be taken care of by appointing agents who spied on their colleagues.

Espionage in foreign countries was given great significance. Intelligent and resourceful agents would be appointed to gather information in the courts not only of enemy kings but also of neutral and friendly ones. Their officials would be under constant watch too. The intriguing aspect lies in the selection of individuals and the specific locations for their use. Hunchbacks, dwarfs, eunuchs, mutes, maids even foreigners would work inside people's houses. Traders and their networks would operate within cities, while ascetics covered the outskirts. The countryside would be the domain of farmers and monks, while forests would be watched by forest-dwellers and people who worked there, like woodcutters. Herdsmen would be employed to keep an eye on the frontier.

The presence of enemy agents within the country was also taken into account and agents were appointed to link up with suspected spies and identify and expose them. They could be highly placed officials who would put up an act of being disaffected and thus trap the enemy into exposing himself.

The spies of the head of the treasury would similarly keep an eye on officials who might be taking bribes and amassing wealth secretly. These would be people who had knowledge and expertise in the job the official was performing.

WHO IS FOR REAL?

It appears that there was widespread use of spies during Kautilya's time, considering the long list of professional covers suggested for them. Not only commonplace ones like those of farmers, traders, doctors and teachers, but the different categories of holy men from monks to priests, wandering ascetics to astrologers and readers of the Puranas. Household

help like cooks and water carriers, entertainers like dancers, actors, storytellers, conjurers and acrobats and even stable hands. Elephant handlers and foresters could be undercover operators. Women agents might adopt the disguise of *parivrajikas* or wandering nuns, rich widows, musicians and maids. It almost sounds like it would be hard to trust anyone you encountered!

THE MATTER OF APPOINTING SPIES

Spies were recruited according to their abilities and their personal needs were also a factor. As is stated, 'Honest and intelligent persons shall be recruited to act as spies.'

It is interesting to take note of the instructions that the Arthashastra shares to ensure that the whole network functions efficiently. For example, a genuine ascetic who wanted to make more money by spying would be appointed a *samastha*. He would take up residence near a city and gather a group of disciples who would adopt guises like those of ascetics with matted hair or shaved heads. They would practice the usual austerities, like fasting, to provide credibility to their cover. However, they would do this in public but fill their bellies in secret.

Other agents would spread the word about the head ascetic's spiritual powers. Those who posed as merchants and traders would put on an act to consult him for advice, while his disciples would sing praises of his occult powers to the skies. When the common people would come to seek his help, he would read palms and make predictions based on the information his network would collect for him. His disciples would make signs and gestures to guide him, and he would foretell all kinds of happenings which the spies from his group would make come true in order to further strengthen his reputation.

The network would use these meetings to pass on information without arousing suspicion.

The Arthashastra also suggests that wandering agents can be recruited from among the orphans who are wards of the state. They can be taught how to understand the meanings of certain gestures, interpret body marks, practise palmistry, perform magic tricks and decipher omens. They would also learn how to conduct themselves in social settings, mastering the art of influencing and winning over people to effectively extract valuable information for their job.

The category of assassins was to be chosen carefully. They had to be extremely courageous but also eager to make money. They had to be 'willing to fight elephants and tigers in total disregard of their personal safety'. In other words, reckless people were considered best for this job.

It is interesting to note that the Arthashastra focuses on the use of a person's natural inclinations in judging their suitability for a particular job.

Financial need is always at the forefront when recruiting agents. For the class of wandering nuns, it is advised that impoverished but courageous widows in need of work should be employed. It is also stressed that they be treated with respect in the palace so that the top officers of the realm readily allow them access to their homes. This will enable these women to gather information about the official's loyalty to the ruler, his sincerity to his duties and his personal habits. Such information could be used in several ways.

Women spies have made an important contribution both in times of war and peace. The First World War spy Mata Hari, a Dutch dancer who spied for Germany, is the most famous one. Noor Inayat Khan, an Indian woman, became a wireless operator during the Second World War and went undercover in occupied France, helping many airmen to escape. She was captured and executed by the Germans. The British awarded her the George Cross, the highest civilian honour. During the freedom movement, Saraswathi Rajamani joined the intelligence wing of Subhas Chandra Bose's Indian National Army and became its youngest member, performing many daring feats. Sehmat Khan, whose life inspired the Bollywood film *Raazi*, was a real-life secret agent who played a crucial role during the Indo-Pak War of 1971.

The roaming agents would pass on all the information to the head agent, who would send it further in code. As is the practice in modern spy networks, the identity of the person who gathered the intelligence would not be disclosed to the one who was to transmit it. Various methods were suggested in case sending prized data became tricky. The agents could use songs and secret signs, place messages in code inside musical instruments or in pots and pans. They could use a variety of disguises as well. If an agent could not easily leave the house where they were collecting information, they were advised to feign illness or madness and rush out.

Along with their various duties, it was the business of the secret agents to foil the efforts of spies working for foreign powers, keep a watch on disaffected elements who might provoke others to rise against the government and find ways to demoralize any enemies within the country. The foreign agents would also work to dilute the strength of hostile nations.

All this shows that the workings of the spy system in ancient India were not that different from those of countries in modern times, apart from the fact that they did not have access to technology and had to depend entirely on well-trained and efficient manpower.

CHAPTER 8

FOREIGN POLICY–ALLIES AND ENEMIES, WAR AND PEACE

What do we mean by foreign policy? In simple terms, it's a government's plan for dealing with other countries in the world, considering the safety of the nation and the well-being of its citizens. Just as having many friends is helpful for an individual, it's also essential for a country to have friendly relations with several nations. These relationships promote peace and enable citizens to lead comfortable lives and make progress. Nevertheless, there will always be countries with whom there are conflicting interests. Hence, having the support of allies is vital when dealing with hostile activities from such enemy countries.

It is interesting to note that in the Arthashastra, the basic principles of a sound foreign policy are not too different from those we follow today. Using diplomacy to create a network of allies with similar goals, while building military power and balancing equations with states weaker or more powerful—both these are aspects of foreign policy that Kautilya discussed. He considered sending envoys to other countries and receiving theirs as an essential part of building a circle of allies who would support the kingdom when it was under attack from a hostile king. He also discussed the importance of maintaining good relations with both smaller and larger countries and using diplomacy, aid and military force as required. Most significantly, this was not a fixed but a dynamic policy that emphasized changing equations with other countries according to the prevailing situation. We must also remember that Kautilya formulated his theories keeping the kingdoms within the region of the Indian sub-continent in mind. In that era, it was pointless to take the world far beyond this area into consideration. In our times, foreign policy has become far more complex since relationships with numerous countries all over the world have to be managed and economic factors like commerce and trade relations come into the picture. However, the basic ideas remain the same.

These principles are incorporated in what has become widely known as Kautilya's *rajamandala* or 'circle of kings' theory. The mandala theory was first conceptualized by Manu the lawmaker as the basis of foreign policy in ancient India but it was Kautilya who developed it as an essential guide to the security and survival of a state.

Kautilya observed that power rises from the strength of the ruler and this power leads to success, and success leads to happiness and the welfare of the people. In his time, expanding his domain was considered the hallmark of a successful ruler. Therefore, he envisaged the king as a conqueror or *vijigishu* who plans to establish his sovereignty over other monarchs while being aware that he is surrounded by friends, enemies and neutral or indifferent rulers. All of whom will possess different levels of power.

MANDALA

Kautilya categorized kings with reference to the complex powerplay between kingdoms based on geographical location, military strength and local conditions. He believed that a neighbour was a natural enemy and that the enemy's enemy was a natural friend.

Kautilya's famous mandala theory listed four circles of kings as a guide to the monarch. The first circle consisted of the conqueror, his friend or *mitra* and his friend's ally or *mitramitra*. The second circle comprised his enemy or *ari*, his enemy's friend or *arimitra* and his friend's ally or *arimitramitra*. The third circle contained the middle king or *madhyama*, his friend and his friend's ally. The fourth circle consisted of the neutral king or *udasina*, his friend and his friend's ally.

The middle king was the one who shared a border with both adversaries and was more powerful than either of them. The neutral king ewas one whose territory did not border either the conqueror's, his enemy's or the middle king's. Thus he was out of the war zone. He was stronger than these three and possessed the ability to support any of them or vanquish them when they were divided. Of course, it was not necessary for such kings to have existed, but in case they did, their response to the conflict would affect the outcome.

A ruler could choose to ally himself with a particular king or stay neutral, and all this would have an important effect on his fate and that of his people.

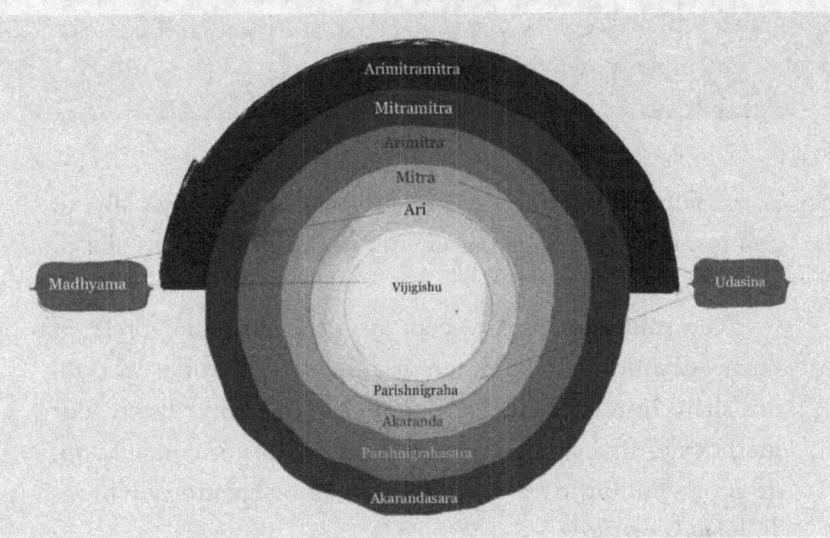

The conqueror is advised to envision the circle of states as a wheel with himself as the hub and his allies as the rim while being separated by the enemy's territory in between. The enemy can be weakened by being hemmed in on both sides. A circle of reliable allies should be established in front and behind the conqueror to strengthen his position like the

In modern times, the situation is more complicated. India has been at war with China in the past and territorial disputes remain. but there are also diplomatic, cultural and trade ties between the two countries. So, in that sense we cannot describe China as the natural enemy. Some scholars consider China the middle king. Pakistan is the best example of a natural enemy. The US can be considered the neutral king from India's point of view.

akaranda or ally in the rear and *akarandasara*, the ally's ally, to counter the *parshnigraha* or enemy in the rear and his ally or *parshnigrahasara*.

Returning to the concept of managing the circle of kings—the hostile neighbours and the friendly rulers who do not share borders with the conqueror—Kautilya listed four methods for managing his relationships: *sama* or conciliation, *dana* or winning over with gifts, *bheda* or creating divisions and *danda* or force.

Kautilya also continued to reiterate that economic power was the propeller of military power. If we were to examine the current global situation, which state would one consider as the most powerful in the world? It is generally accepted that the US qualifies for this position, though China is striving to make its presence felt on the global scene. The US has the strongest military, its economy is the most stable and its citizens enjoy a high standard of living. How did it achieve this status? The fact is that the US achieved paramountcy after World War II when UK and other European countries were weakened by the financial fallout of a long war that drained their resources. While the European economy was in a shambles, the USA, which had not suffered much damage, developed its industries considerably, eventually becoming a global superpower.

Kautilya also stated that not all rulers would be interested in expanding their kingdoms. But even if they wished to live in peace, their neighbours could have other plans. Every kingdom was vulnerable to attack from more ambitious monarchs, whether in its neighbourhood or distant lands. Thus, for the sake of sheer self-protection, a wise ruler had to follow a foreign policy that guaranteed the safety of his people and enabled him to hold on to his throne.

With this in mind, Kautilya defined six principles for an effective foreign policy. These were:

1. The king should encourage progress in all fields to gain prosperity and stockpile the resources for his military campaigns.
2. He must use all his resources to defeat his enemy.
3. He must maintain good relationships with his allies.
4. He must always follow a prudent course of action.
5. He should always choose peace over war.
6. The king should always remain just, whether in victory or defeat.

Kautilya mentioned that it is important to crush an enemy kingdom to eliminate the threat to the stability of one's own country. He did not believe in negotiating with the 'natural enemy'—the neighbouring kingdom, which had plans to grab the conqueror's territory. There could be other neighbours who were hostile but did not pose the same threat. Some could be friendly, and some could be subject states. It was also not necessary that the enemy state might share boundaries; there could be a small state in between that acted as a buffer. Again, Kautilya advised that the king was not to declare his warlike intentions openly. Diplomatic relations were to be maintained with the enemy. War was to be declared when the conditions were suitable and victory was reasonably assured. The king was to possess sufficient funds, the army was to be well-prepared, or the enemy was to have been weakened by internal or external strife or any other situation that makes the declaration effective.

Kautilya gave much weight to good relations with allies, going so far as to describe them as a 'constituent element of a state', the only external element. Providing help was considered the most important aspect of an alliance between states, as was trust. A former ally who broke a treaty and joined the enemy was deemed worse than the enemy itself. 'Even an enemy who helps is fit to be allied with, not an ally who does not act like one.'

Kautilya warned against waging a reckless war just because a king was ambitious for power. If the country was making good progress, it was better to keep the peace. War created unnecessary expenditure; men could lose their lives and leave their homes and families which would affect their morale. However, when a treaty was being negotiated, and the terms were not just and beneficial, it was better to keep fighting. It was also preferable for the weaker king to sue for peace if the enemy is at his gates and he were unable to defend himself. The Arthashastra does say that when making peace does not alter the balance between two rulers, it is preferable to make a treaty—one that attempts to cover all kinds of situations.

After Alexander the Great's death, Seleucus Nikator, the general who took control of the eastern part of his empire, waged war against Chandragupta. However, he suffered defeat and eventually entered into a treaty in 305 BCE. It is said that Chandragupta either married Seleucus's daughter or niece. Following this, the Greek ruler dispatched several envoys, including Megasthenes, to the Mauryan court, who left behind accounts of life at the Mauryan court.

As a gesture of goodwill, Chandragupta presented Seleucus with 500 elephants, which greatly aided him in his future wars. This agreement serves as an excellent example of how diplomacy can foster friendly relations between two nations that were once at war.

Kautilya elaborated further on his six principles by defining different situations like peace or *samdhi*, war or *vigraha*, deliberate inactivity or *asana*, *yana* or preparing for war, seeking the protection of a more powerful ruler when attacked or *samasraya*, making an alliance with one king to attack another, essentially a dual policy or *dwaidhibhava*. The wise king was to decide the right approach after weighing his options.

Keeping Peace

Kautilya also goes into detail about the different aspects of making, keeping, violating and renegotiating a treaty.

Soon after India gained independence, it was faced with a difficult choice. The end of the Second World War in 1945 led to the formation of two major power blocs in the world—the USA and its allies called the capitalist Western Bloc and the USSR and its satellite nations and supporters or the communist Eastern Bloc. This resulted in the Cold War, during which the two Blocs were in conflict but there was no open war. Both sides tried to draw the other countries of the world into their respective orbits. It was a tricky situation for our new country. Jawaharlal Nehru and the other leaders felt that it was important to guard our independence and sovereignty and decided to follow the path of non-alignment. India first used this term along with Yugoslavia at the United Nations in 1950 when they refused to back any side during the Korean War between North and South Korea. A series of conferences led to the formation of the Non-Aligned Movement (NAM) in 1956 and Nehru was among its first signatories along with President Josip Broz Tito of Yugoslavia and Gamel Abdel Nassar of Egypt. This policy was part of an attempt to focus on developing the country and to avoid being under the shadow of the new imperialism. Incidentally, Nehru had great admiration for Kautilya and the Arthashastra and was guided by the concept of putting your country's interests first. However, it is worth noting that during the Indo-Pak War of 1971, none of the NAM countries supported India.

The Six Methods of Achieving Progress

According to the Arthashastra, the aim of the king is to make progress and six methods of foreign policy are suggested to accomplish this objective. Each of these will, of course, apply under different circumstances.

1. Making peace

The king is advised to make peace when he and his enemy are equally balanced, or when he feels it's important to focus on developing and augmenting his resources, or is able to erode the enemy's power secretly.

2. Waging war

The king can achieve progress by waging war when he is confident of victory because he has a strong and well-equipped army, is strategically well-placed and the enemy is in a weakened position.

3. Staying quiet

A king can also make progress by staying quiet—that is neither making war nor seeking to make peace in a situation when both he and his enemy are so firmly placed that they can't harm each other or the enemy is tied up coping with a disaster or some other conflict which allows the king to focus on growing his own resources.

4. Preparing for war

A king can achieve progress by preparing for war if he can ensure the security of his own resources while destroying those of the enemy.

5. Seeking support

If the king is unable to destroy the enemy's resources or protect his own from attack, he should seek help from a stronger king. This will allow him to avoid defeat and he can try to strengthen his position in the meantime.

6. Pursuing a dual policy

A king can also save his own resources by making peace with one enemy while waging war with another.

Kautilya further cautioned that the would-be-conqueror needs to apply these methods judiciously, taking his own power into account.

He should make peace with an enemy equal in power or one who is stronger and wage war on a weaker king. He uses the analogy of a foot soldier fighting an elephant for a king taking on a stronger opponent.

The pauses or periods of inaction between war and peace are discussed too. These are long periods of inaction, inaction for a definite reason and intentionally refraining from action. A long period of inactivity is required when there is an internal crisis which affects the king's ability to wage a successful war. Inaction for a purpose implies waiting for a favourable chance to attack the enemy. The king may deliberately avoid action even if the opportunity is there to make war or peace.

Kautilya advised that if it so happened that neither party could inflict casualties, it was better to halt operations or make peace. According to him, a king should declare war but then halt operations under the following conditions:

a) When he finds that he can overcome another ruler who is equally or more powerful with the help of allies.
b) His citizens are courageous, united and well-off and are strong enough to inflict damage on the enemy.
c) The enemy's citizens are prepared to change sides, whether on their own or with the use of incentives because they are dissatisfied, ill-treated, poverty-stricken, avaricious and insecure.
d) If his own country is well-off while that of his opponent is suffering want, which makes it likely for the people to support him.
e) In the opposite situation—when his own people are suffering deprivation and their loyalties are uncertain—in that case he can offer the inducement of plundering the enemy's grain, cattle and gold.
f) He can stop the import of the enemy's produce into his own country, which will affect their prosperity.
g) The war conditions allow him to channel valuable goods of the enemy from a particular trade route.

h) The war prevents the enemy from dealing with disaffected elements in his own country, like treacherous people, his opponents and the jungle tribes in his country.

Kautilya further suggested that a king should declare war and wait till the time his enemy attacked an ally because a victory would empower him further. By supporting his ally, the king would not only demonstrate his own courage but also cement his relationship with the ally, who would come to his help later.

In the event that declaring war and waiting did not yield a favourable result, the king was to make peace.

Kautilya also gave detailed instructions on resuming hostilities after a period of waiting.

Further, he said that the king was to take action only when his allies in the front and behind him were supported by courageous, well-off subjects and the enemy and his allies were not in good condition.

Kautilya advised on which state the conqueror should target. He said that if there were two countries equally afflicted with disasters and thus vulnerable, the king was to first attack his natural enemy or one whose subjects were disaffected. After subduing this enemy, the king was to target the other vulnerable one.

He pointed out that alliances could be as complicated as hostility and a friendship with a more powerful king had its own risks, except when one was actually at war. The king was to always ask a king stronger than his enemy for protection. When he sought support and the choice was between a king he loved and one who loved him, he was supposed to ally with the one who loved him. At the same time, Kautilya gave space to the exceptions. In case there was no king stronger than the enemy, the conqueror was to make peace, even if it was temporary, till his position was more secure.

When he needed protection and was faced with two more powerful kings, he was to seek out the one who was more efficient or one who could act as a buffer. When he had to back both, he was to make the excuse of financial hardship while trying to divide them with implications that one was conspiring against the other. Once relationships deteriorated between them, the king was to continue making the situation worse and destroy them turn by turn using secret warfare.

A conqueror who had two strong kings in his vicinity needed to be vigilant. He could stay safe in a well-defended fort and ally himself with one of the kings, while being unfriendly towards the other. He could also act according to the needs of his situation after weighing the benefits of war and peace.

For the purpose of weakening his rivals, the conqueror could make use of defectors—subjects antagonistic to the other king and jungle chiefs. He could then ally with one to reduce the other's power. We notice this in current times too when a country supports separatist movements to weaken another.

If the conqueror was being threatened by both of them, he was to turn to his circle of kings for support—the middle king or the neutral king—and try to team up with one adversary to eliminate the other or attempt to eliminate both of them. When the US backed Pakistan as a buffer state during the Cold War, India maintained cordial relations with the Soviet Union.

If two kings managed to get together to defeat the conqueror, he was to seek refuge with a principled ruler among the middle or neutral kings or one who was in their circle.

The Role of Envoys

One part of foreign policy deals with war and peace and the other discusses fostering good relations with other countries using envoys.

When we describe someone as being very diplomatic, it implies that the individual is remarkably tactful and skilled at engaging with others in a pleasant manner, even having the ability to pacify belligerent individuals. The term is derived from 'diplomat'—a person adept at persuading individuals with differing or conflicting perspectives to reach a consensus. No wonder that officials who represent their country in a foreign land are called diplomats because their ability to assess the mood of another ruler and build up friendship is invaluable in cementing relations between the countries.

The role of envoys is considered important in the Arthashastra. Today those who join the Indian Foreign Service are selected among the top-rank holders of the civil services exam but as mentioned earlier, such exams didn't exist in ancient India.

Kautilya advised that envoys should be selected after the king had decided on a certain policy after discussing it with his councillors. He listed the duties of the envoys and cautioned that the envoys should be kept under surveillance by spies, visible and invisible guards and counter-envoys.

Much the way that diplomats in contemporary times have different ranks and responsibilities, Kautilya suggested that envoys were to belong to various categories.

The plenipotentiary or top envoy, whom we refer to as an ambassador today, had to be a person who possessed the qualities of a counsellor or amatya in the government. He would have complete authority to represent the king and negotiate on his behalf. One with three-quarters of the credentials could only be sent on a restricted assignment. And one with half the qualifications could only act as a messenger.

The envoy had several duties to perform, and he was expected to fulfil them meticulously. He would pass on relevant information to his king about the kingdom where he was stationed and make sure that the terms of any treaty were being upheld. He had to maintain the honour of the king through appropriate behaviour and actions, seek out support for his country, create discord among the friends of their enemies, send spies and forces into enemy territory and entice the enemy king's relatives to back his ruler.

Kautilya stressed on the importance of preparing efficiently for the mission. The envoy was expected to be a person of superior abilities, and his planning had to be meticulous. He had to begin his journey in a thoroughly organized manner by putting together the required vehicles, draught animals and a retinue of servants. Thus, he would have impressed the other ruler by demonstrating the status and resources of his king.

The envoy's mission began the moment he left the court. During his journey, he was expected to create good contacts among jungle chiefs, frontier officers and chief officers of the cities and countryside. He had to take note of suitable positions for placing forces both in his country and that of the other king, along with strategic locations for doing battle, support facilities and backup spots for emergencies.

He had to observe a particular etiquette when he arrived at his destination. He was to present himself to the king only after he had received the go-ahead to do so, and he was supposed to convey the message in exactly the same language he had been briefed in, even if it meant putting himself at risk.

According to the Shastras, an envoy was not to be killed, under any circumstances. Even today, the concept of 'diplomatic immunity' exists, which means envoys have certain rights and are not subject to all the local laws.

The envoy could not leave his post unless he received orders from his ruler, but if he feared that he might be held captive or that his life was in danger, he could depart without permission.

If an envoy did not leave after delivering an unpleasant message, he could be held captive.

When the envoy's stay was extended because he had not been allowed to leave, there were certain rules he had to observe. He had to be extremely discreet and balanced in his behaviour and not let any polite and respectful treatment he received affect his judgement.

The emissary was also expected to recruit double agents who could pass off as merchants, ascetics and their disciples, physicians or heretics in order to discover the best way to instigate the disloyal people in the court, win over those who were faithful to their ruler and find out how devoted the king's subjects were to him and what the vulnerable points of the kingdom were.

He had to be careful not to give away information about his own king—either his strong points or his fallibilities. If questioned directly by the other ruler, he was to give evasive answers or such that furthered his king's agenda.

In a situation where the envoy's mission had not been successful and he was still not allowed to depart, he had to try and gauge the king's reasons for not letting him go.

Once he had assessed the reason, the envoy was to make his decision to either depart or request an explanation from the king.

What are Treaties?

Treaties are a very important part of international relations, whether they are negotiated at the end of a war, are about recognizing mutual boundaries or for the purposes of an alliance between two or more countries.

In contemporary times, treaties are deliberated upon, witnessed by many people and considered legally binding according to international law. How were they approached in ancient India? Kautilya wrote extensively on the categories of treaties, which kinds were favourable with regard to a king's progress and how they were to be enforced. As in his other theories, his approach was based on the practise of dharma as well as his pragmatic understanding of human behaviour.

Treaties were mostly verbal agreements at that time. A king's word was supposed to be enough. But not every ruler could be relied upon to stick to the terms. Thus, it was the practice to give a hostage to guarantee that the treaty would be upheld. If the treaty was violated, the hostage would lose his life. Kautilya did not look upon such treaties favourably.

When there was suspicion about the intentions of a particular party, highly respected men, ascetics or chiefs would stand as a guarantee to uphold it. In such events, the king who managed to get a guarantor who had some control over the other party got the upper hand.

Kautilya defined treaties as those which had no particular conditions and those in which these were specified.

A treaty without conditions would be made when a king wanted to outsmart an opponent who was evil, lazy, lacked foresight and patience. It could be a simple alliance which would help the king ascertain the other's weaknesses and declare war when the time was ripe.

Regarding treaties with conditions, Kautilya listed seven types of such treaties. They could specify either the place, time, and objective individually, or a combination of any two, or all three together. A treaty concerning place meant that two parties would agree to attack distinct regions.

A treaty concerning time was one where the period of the campaign was predetermined. This treaty was made when the other king's conquests would have adverse consequences for him while the conqueror's gains would be more stable.

A treaty about objectives was one in which the two parties proclaimed their aims in conducting a campaign. This agreement was to be made when the end gains of the war would not be beneficial for the other king, but the conqueror would achieve lasting benefits.

The Arthashastra suggested that in case of a treaty with conditions, the conqueror should take prompt action and put obstacles in the way of his enemy.

There were also unconcealed treaties in which there was no hidden agenda; everything was straightforward.

Since Kautilya had attempted to cover all angles, the possible response of the conqueror's enemy was also set forth.

RENEGOTIATING TREATIES

According to Kautilya's view, fear, lack of activity and resentment were the only reasons that could lead a vassal or an ally to part ways with the conqueror.

A party that decided to end an agreement may have wanted to reconsider their decision later. In such cases, the treaty had to be renegotiated. Typically, the normal course of action would be to take up arms against a vassal or ally who had dishonoured a treaty and defeat them. However, there were instances where this approach could be reconsidered after examining the reasons for the party's return. The Arthashastra advised the conqueror to entertain the ally who had abandoned him for good reasons and also returned to him for justifiable reasons. It also recommended renegotiating an agreement with one who had acted against his enemy. However, on no condition was he to consider the overtures of the person who abandoned him without any valid cause and tried to patch up without any worthwhile reasons. Similarly, a king who had acted against the conqueror's interests was to be rejected.

In the case of a former ally who had acted against both the conqueror and his enemy and left for justifiable reasons but returned to pursue his own interests, it was advised to scrutinize his motives carefully.

If a returning ally's motives were found to be sincere, then he would receive a warm welcome. Otherwise, he was to be shunned. Kautilya further advised that the ally who had acted against both the conqueror and his enemy but returned to make peace for the right reasons needed to be examined too.

There were situations when the conqueror might have been compelled to renegotiate a treaty despite adverse conditions. In such a case, the king could have patched up relations but remained cautious in his interactions, giving due consideration to the other party's military and economic strength.

EQUAL AND UNEQUAL TREATIES

As mentioned earlier, treaties are not always equal in nature because the power of the negotiating parties may not be equally balanced. But who makes the first move? It can be either party, but the bargaining process would be different. Kautilya mentioned three different situations—negotiations between rulers equal in might, overtures made by the weaker king to the stronger and vice versa.

Different conditions could affect the outcome of the discussions. There could have been natural disasters or other losses compelling a king to accept an unequal treaty. However, if both sides trusted each other, an unequal treaty could have been ratified. If there was a deficiency of belief, the offer would have been considered an inimical gesture. Keeping this hypothetical situation in mind, Kautilya suggested that a king equal in stature should be given the exact value, the weaker king less and the stronger king more.

However, each situation was not that straightforward, and Kautilya elaborated on the different kinds of unequal treaties. He defined an unequal treaty as one in which the equal, weaker or stronger king did not receive conditions in proportion to his power.

An exceptionally unequal treaty was one in which one of the parties received a disproportionate advantage.

Kautilya further advised that if the treaty was justly balanced, peace was to be made. When the benefits were one-sided, it was better to make war.

UNEQUAL TREATIES–PRESENT AND FUTURE GAIN

Kautilya went deeper into the complex aspects of making treaties. The process went beyond simply balancing the figures for payment for troops and the number and quality of fighting men for which payment was made. The total gain had to be considered; not just the immediate benefit but the future ones too. In some situations, it might have been worth it to forgo any obvious gain to save the advantage for another time. In addition, he also gave suggestions about the appropriate time to ask for payment.

When the conqueror was facing a cash crunch or if he did not trust the other party, it would have been advisable to accept a small advantage to gain a larger one later, when it suited him. A situation could also arise when both the conqueror and his enemy tried to support the same party—a neighbour, the middle king or the neutral king. In this case, the party that proved to be the better ally would have won over his enemy. As Kautilya pointed out with his usual pragmatism, friends had to be helped because they would help you in turn, thus furthering your own cause. When you supported a party that was actually closer to your enemy, you stood to lose not only financially but also by being away from your court, and you might have ended up earning the hatred of the other party who might have resented your assistance. Similarly, when the middle or neutral king received support from the conqueror and turned hostile, it meant that the enemy had scored over him. In the event of helping the middle or neutral king with troops, the party who supplied better trained and equipped, more courageous and loyal troops was considered to have gotten the upper hand over his enemy.

THE WEAKER KING

Kautilya discussed the situation of a king who was under attack from a stronger adversary. The weaker king could request support from a more powerful ruler or take shelter in a fort if possible. An agreement had to be made with the king whose protection he sought. Kautilya categorized the kinds of treaties that the weaker king could make based on the conditions. For example, if his troops were offered to the protector, or his treasure, or if land was being ceded. He advised the weak king to surrender in case of an attack and offer his person as hostage or his army, treasury or territory.

Three kinds of treaties were suggested, considering the king's situation, place and time:

i)   A treaty in which he gave himself up as a hostage along with a certain number of troops.
ii) A treaty with another hostage, like the crown prince or chief of defence, along with a specific number of troops, while the king remained free.
iii) A treaty without hostages where the king and his army retreated to another place to escape.

Kautilya further suggested that in the first two instances, a marital alliance could be made with a highly placed person on his side, either the crown prince or the chief of defence, with a woman from the stronger king's family.

The next kind of treaty involved a financial settlement, and Kautilya had some interesting suggestions about such agreements. These are listed as four different kinds:

i)   The first was the buying-off treaty in which the king surrendered his treasury to effect the release of captives or the safety of his people.

ii) A treaty of tribute, where payments were made over a length of time, or it was specified that the tribute in cash or particular products would be given in a certain number of instalments at specific times and places.

iii) A golden treaty, based on trust and good relations, in which the terms of tribute were not harsh and immediate payment was not demanded was considered superior to a treaty based on a marriage alliance.

iv) The beggaring treaty was just the opposite where an immediate and unreasonable amount of tribute was demanded.

Kautilya suggested that in the first two kinds of treaties, the tribute should consist of forest produce or poisoned elephants and horses. The third kind should be honoured sincerely, and in the last case, the excuse of destitution could be made to defer the payment.

Kautilya also classified the treaties in which territory had to be ceded into four categories:

i)   A treaty of cession in which a portion of the territory was ceded to save the rest of the kingdom. This was better when the part that was ceded was rife with secret agents and robbers.

ii) A scorched earth treaty in which the land to be surrendered was stripped of its resources, made by a king who wished disasters to befall his enemy.

iii) A lease treaty in which the land was retained by giving up all its produce to the other party.

iv) A ruinous treaty in which the amount of tribute expected was greater than what the land could produce.

Kautilya advised that in the case of the first two kinds of treaties, the weaker king should try and recapture the territory, whereas in the last two, he should attempt to save the produce for himself.

Treaties can change the fate of nations. The Treaty of Allahabad signed in 1765 between the Mughal Emperor Shah Alam II and Robert Clive of the East India Company after the Battle of Buxar gave the British a political and constitutional foothold in India. They were given the *diwani* or power to collect taxes in Bengal, Bihar and Orissa on behalf of Shah Alam, which gave them immense administrative power.

HOSTAGES

It seems that giving hostages was a regular feature in negotiating treaties at that time. Kautilya considered this kind of treaty the least satisfactory one. According to him, treaties based on dharma were the most acceptable. However, he accepted the realities of his time and human nature and devoted an entire chapter to hostages. This also included the rescue of the hostage, which implied that such a treaty did not have such a strong foundation as those based on word of honour or swearing an oath. It implied mutual distrust from the beginning. As in most cases, hostages were exchanged as a way to secure the faithful execution of the treaty.

ALLIES AND VASSAL KINGS

Kautilya discussed the relationships with the allies and vassal kings of the conqueror at length too. Allies were rulers who had a special bond with the conqueror or a common cause with him. This could be a common enemy with whom they shared borders. Vassal kings were those who had been subjugated but had received honourable treatment, so they owed fealty to him. Earlier Kautilya had stated the good qualities of a desirable ally as one who had capability was reliable, industrious and firm and also possessed the loyalty of his subjects.

When making alliances, what qualities should the king seek? According to Kautilya, to control the ally, he had to be reliable in friendship, raise a force in stealth and have troops amassed in one place. He also considered a gift of territory as the best support. Financial aid and manpower came next in order.

Where a vassal king was concerned, Kautilya advised giving land to a neighbouring king who could have turned hostile, but not land that would have yielded much profit in any way.

If a vassal king proved treacherous, he was to be done away with, either publicly or in a clandestine manner, but the loyal vassal was to be treated with courtesy. The king who surrendered should have been dealt with honourably too, and his family should have also received just treatment.

At the same time, Kautilya was well aware of the unpredictability of allies—in a power struggle, friendship was easily strained. He listed the categories of kings who were not going to be reliable allies:

1. An ally who attacked another of the conqueror's allies along with another party and was under that king's influence.
2. A king who abandoned an alliance to make another or due to weakness or avarice.
3. A king who succumbed to an enemy's bribe and left the alliance.
4. A king who did not stick to the original agreement of attacking one party and making peace with another but

adopted a different course of action by attacking another enemy.

5. A king who joined another campaign after promising to support the conqueror or left him to fight his own battle.
6. One who had been forced out of his kingdom or left it under threat.
7. One who had undergone the humiliation of being deprived of his possessions, denied what is rightfully his, and compelled to receive unwanted things.
8. One who had been compelled to pay tribute or agreed to pay an excessive amount.
9. One who had joined the enemy because he failed to accomplish a task beyond his powers.
10. One who had been overlooked because he did not seem a strong enough ally earlier.
11. One who did not entertain requests for an alliance.

Kautilya also categorized the kings who would make desirable allies. He said that certain alliances were likely to endure because the kings in question would be dependable.

1. One who put in efforts to maintain the alliance.
2. One whose bearing and actions commanded respect.
3. One who had become alienated due to misunderstanding or treacherous individuals creating a chasm.
4. One who had not received due respect from the conqueror's enemy.

5. One whose progress had been hampered by the designs of the enemy.
6. One who feared that his enemies might gang up against him.

Kautilya added that a wise king would take measures to prevent any harm befalling his allies. In such an event, he would take immediate action to come to their aid.

The qualities of the best ally have also been mentioned. 'The best ally is one who possesses the following six qualities: being a longstanding ally of the family, unwavering in loyalty, amenable to control, providing robust support, sharing common interests, capable of swift mobilization of forces and never betraying his friends.'

All allies are not the same, and Kautilya cautioned the conqueror against taking his friends for granted.

The USA can be regarded as a reliable ally to the UK, as it provided support during both the First and Second World Wars. These two nations share a unique and special relationship. In Medieval Europe, Christian countries engaged in the Crusades to counter Muslim expansion. King Francis I of France, however, displayed unreliability as an ally when he reached an agreement with Suleyman I, the Ottoman

Emperor of Turkey, in 1536, against his fellow Christian ruler, the Holy Roman Emperor Charles V.

During the Second World War, Switzerland remained neutral and could be characterized as a disinterested ally, facilitating communication between the warring factions. Initially neutral, the USA formally entered the conflict in 1941 after the Japanese attack on Pearl Harbor, making it the final type of ally in that scenario.

According to him, a reliable ally is one who shares similar goals, provides ready assistance, and remains steadfast without backstabbing even during the conqueror's difficult times. On the other hand, an unreliable ally switches loyalties between the king and his enemy. A disinterested ally maintains good relations with both the king and his enemy but lacks commitment to either. Additionally, an ally with substantial and productive territory, power and contentment in what he owns may not be inclined to aid the king in times of trouble.

An ally who is weak and has received support from both the king and the enemy will remain neutral in a conflict. Another type of ally, inherently hostile to the conqueror but forced to align due to being caught between powerful rulers, lacks the capability and commitment to provide support. A hostile ally, closer to the enemy and obligated to them, may offer support but poses a potential threat. Finally, a dangerous ally abandons the conqueror and later attempts to reconcile, posing a threat to the conqueror's life. While taking stock of the characteristics of different allies, Kautilya also pointed out the benefits of having allies. There could be an ally who supported the king in numerous ways—whether it was his agricultural produce from his fields and herds, or goods from trade, the produce of his mines, gems and other articles of high and low value, the produce of his forests, animals for transport and vehicles. Another useful ally was one who came to the king's aid with forces and money. The ally who supported the king with troops, money and land was an all-around friend. The one who put up a resistance against the king's enemy was defined as an ally on one side, while one who battled both the enemy and the enemy's ally was described as an ally on two sides. The one who confronted the enemy, his ally, his neighbour and the jungle tribe was considered the ally on all sides.

Thus, Kautilya summed up both the strength and commitment of different allies through these definitions.

World leaders frequently demonstrate goodwill towards each other through friendly gestures such as exchanging gifts or showcasing warm handshakes and embraces in the media. Kautilya acknowledged that alliances are not solely driven by self-interest and political necessity. He highlighted the significance of enduring friendships, stating, 'That friend whose friendship has endured since earlier times, and who protects and is in turn protected out of love and not for mercenary reasons, is called a constant ally.' However, the truth is that not many alliances are based on genuine friendship. There is also the important question of binding an ally to you because you have some leverage over him. Consequently, the Arthashastra categorized allies as those who could be controlled or not. For example, an ally who might have received or provided aid and acted consistently against the conqueror's enemy but had a powerful stronghold like an impregnable fort or forest retreat could have been labelled a constant ally who was not amenable to control. On the other hand, an ally who joined forces with the conqueror only when he was being invaded or facing some other problem was an ally who could be controlled but could not be said to be steadfast.

This brings us to another question. In circumstances when the conqueror had to choose between two allies, both of whom were in a tight situation, which of these should the king have backed? The one who was consistent but could not be controlled or the one who was likely to be a momentary friend but could be dominated. The opinion of some of the authorities Kautilya quoted was that the permanent ally, who could not be manipulated, should be chosen because even if he was not able to provide too much support, he would not damage the conqueror. But Kautilya felt that the temporary ally would be better because he would stick to the alliance.

Kautilya's pragmatic approach was also evident in all the advice he gave about choosing allies, which often differed from the other experts mentioned in the Arthashastra. When the conqueror had the option to team up with one of two allies, both of whom could be kept in control, but one could give extensive support for a short time while the other could provide small amounts of assistance over an extensive period, who was better? Kautilya differed from the advice of the teachers who recommended the one who could offer substantial support but for a limited period. His argument was that the ally who could provide substantial support might pull out halfway if he felt too much was being expected from him; moreover, he would expect compensation. The ally who continued to give aid, even if it was not considerable, was more reliable in the long run.

Other choices that confronted kings were picking an ally who was powerful but slow in mobilization over one who might have been quick to gather his forces, though he may not have been so strong. Kautilya disagreed with the experts who extolled the virtues of the powerful king because of the status gained by associating with such a king. He said that the ally who could bring forces on to the field aided in taking action at the appropriate time; also, being weaker, he could have been manipulated by the conqueror. Then there was the question of the ally whose troops were disciplined but not concentrated in one place, while another had his forces amassed together but they were unruly. Kautilya recommended the second option because it was easier to inculcate discipline in troops that were gathered, even if they were uncontrollable earlier, by considering their demands.

Kautilya advised the conqueror to always be fair and just towards the kingdoms he had subdued. In this way, he would retain their loyalty for generations to come.

What forms did these policies take?

Sama meant extending a benevolent hand to the inhabitants of villages and forests, protecting cattle herds and trade routes. Also, extraditing subjects who had fallen out with the subject king, were conspiring against him, as well as criminals and wrongdoers who had escaped into the conqueror's territory.

Dana was gifts of land and money and the promise to back the king in the case of attempts to overthrow him.

To prevent the subject king from going over to the enemy, bheda was created by communicating demands of land, money and armed forces as if they came from a neighbour, jungle chief or a member of the king's family who was disgruntled. Thus, he would have remained suspicious of these people and would have reposed trust in the conqueror as his well-wisher.

Danda could have been both open attack on the enemy or irregular warfare that secretly eroded his power.

CHAPTER 9
THE BUSINESS OF MAKING WAR

Since he envisaged the king as a conqueror, Kautilya's foreign policy included waging war to expand territory. Therefore, the Arthashastra goes into detail about the structure of the army and the actual business of war. Kautilya believed that it was crucial for a king to assess his opponent's power before declaring war. This meant economic and military strength as well as intellectual power. He rated intellectual power or the capability to analyse and make correct judgments superior to military strength, even to morale. The king was also to consult his ministers and assess his financial capability, the preparedness of his troops, make sure of his allies and take note of the seasonal and geographical conditions. All these aspects continue to hold weight in modern warfare.

According to Kautilya, there were four categories of war to be waged as per the prevailing situation. *Mantrayuddha* or war by council meant employing diplomacy instead of outright hostility against a stronger enemy. *Prakasayuddha* was war openly declared at a specific time and place, usually against a weaker opponent. *Kutayuddha* was hidden warfare and can also be described as psychological warfare or what we know as guerrilla warfare. The fourth was *gudayuddha* or silent warfare in which secret agents created discord, spread disinformation, and assassinated important officers or the enemy ruler himself.

The Indo-Pak wars of 1965 and 1971 can be described as open war. Examples of guerilla warfare from Indian history are Maharana Pratap's hidden campaign against the Mughal Akbar and Shivaji's attacks on Aurangzeb's general Shaista Khan. The militancy in Kashmir is also described as a guerilla war. Kautilya's concept of silent warfare is considered unique for its time by many military experts. Modern day cyber warfare can be taken as an excellent example of this concept.

To be successful in war, it was crucial for the conqueror to have effective control over his army. Kautilya advised the king to inspect his forces regularly and make every attempt to win their loyalty. The generals and senior officers were to be paid handsome salaries so that they were not tempted to defect to the enemy. The soldiers were to also receive adequate remuneration to keep them satisfied. In addition, secret agents were to watch them for signs of disaffection and treachery. Those officers who appeared to lack courage were to be removed from their posts. For further security, the four wings of the army were to be placed under the command of several generals. This would ensure rivalry among them, which meant that they would keep an eye on each other.

During times of peace, a standing army was to be maintained, sufficient to guard the forts as well as the king's property. The officers in charge of these forces were to be permanent employees but would be frequently transferred. The king's own guards were a special unit which was also permanent. When a war flared up, additional forces could be raised and disbanded later.

When the king had to recruit more troops, he needed extra finances. This could have been accomplished by trading Crown goods. The funds raised were paid to the soldiers to cover the expenses of their families while they were at war.

In contemporary times, methods of warfare are very different from what Kautilya described, however, many of the strategies he advised are still applicable. The four wings of the army mentioned in the Arthashastra reflect the ancient Indian pattern of elephant troops, chariots, horses, and infantry. The actual practice was that on the battlefield, the fighter on horseback was surrounded by six foot-soldiers while the elephants and chariots were surrounded by five units of horses. The infantry consisted of archers along with soldiers armed with swords, spears and lances for hand-to-hand fighting. Apart from the usual land campaigns, the battle could be fought on water as well as in trenches.

Kautilya also categorized the forces as the standing army, the territorial army, the militias, which could be mercenaries, the allied forces, foreign troops and tribal forces.

According to Kautilya, the ideal army was one in which soldiers received an adequate salary, were given due respect by their officers and had their achievements recognized—the way our army today awards medals for bravery. Its strength was to be appropriately maintained and it was to be a tight-knit force of men from similar regions or backgrounds to promote camaraderie at the time of battle. Care had to be taken to weed out traitors and malingerers who might demotivate others. In wartime, whatever happened, the king was not to abandon his army, leaving it leaderless. If a commander was killed in battle, he would have to be replaced immediately. Neither were the native forces to be combined with another kingdom's army. Enough troops were needed to reinforce others when they were beleaguered in battle. The wise king also made sure that the men were not exhausted by long marches that sapped their strength. Additionally, the forces to be used in a battle were trained as required. When outmatched, Kautilya advised that it was better to retreat and save lives.

Similar to what Kautilya suggested, some of the oldest infantry regiments in the Indian Army were recruited from the inhabitants of certain regions or communities like the Kumaon Regiment, the Sikh Regiment, the Rajput Regiment and the Gurkha Rifles, among others.

Kautilya also listed thirty-four different kinds of problems that would prevent an army from performing efficiently. These include some of the reasons mentioned earlier, like soldiers not receiving their salaries, being in poor health, being too exhausted, being forced to fight in the wrong season, being low in morale, left leaderless, angry or disgruntled, disorganized or overwhelmed by a superior force. He considered it sensible practice for the king to give timely payment to his soldiers and take care of their nutrition and health. This is reminiscent of Napoleon's statement that an army marches on its stomach.

The Indian Armed Forces today consist of three main wings—the army, navy and air force. There are also several paramilitary forces that provide additional support. The President is the Supreme Commander, but the prime minister is the executive authority, along with cabinet ministers, while the ministry of defence manages the affairs of the armed forces. The chief of army staff, the chief of naval staff and the chief of air staff head the different wings. India's is the second-largest army in the world after China.

Since horses and elephants were integral parts of an army, their essential qualities are listed too. Thus, Kautilya valued a good pedigree, physical strength, proper training, speed, stamina, valour, an imposing appearance, obedience, as well as auspicious marks.

Kautilya has defined the structure of the army, which begins with the commander-in-chief, most likely the king himself, below whom is the senapati or chief of defence. The next category were the chief commanders heading the elephant corps, the chariot corps, the cavalry and the infantry. They would have divisional commanders below them, and other officers of lower rank.

Each division was to have distinguishing trumpet sounds, flags and banners which would be used to signal specific commands to them.

THE SENAPATI

The senapati played a crucial role, so he had to be highly skilled in the use of all kinds of weapons. He was to also possess great expertise in riding elephants, horses and chariots. Additionally, he was to have accurate knowledge of the strength of the wings of the army and the correct way to use them in battle. It was his responsibility to ensure discipline among the forces, whether the army was camping, marching to battle or fighting. As the head of the armed forces, he had to understand how to choose the best time to set off on a campaign, the right terrain and the best season for a particular attack.

Elephants have been described as the tanks of ancient armies. Alexander the Great, the Carthaginians and even the Mughals used large numbers of elephants in battle. Kautilya believed that a strong elephant corps guaranteed victory for a king.

The chief commander of the elephant corps oversaw catching of suitable elephants from the forests and training them for battle.

The head of the cavalry was expected to be familiar with the characteristics of horses from diverse areas and be proficient in training them.

The chief of the chariot corps had to be an expert in the use of all kinds of weapons. He supervised the charioteers, the attendants and the chariot horses, as well as the manufacture of a variety of chariots.

The chief of the infantry had to be well-informed about the capabilities of the different sections of his troops, ranging from the standing army, the militia, friendly forces, alien and tribal ones. He was expected to be knowledgeable about battle manoeuvres and had to maintain the fitness of his troops both in times of war and peace.

There was also a chief of ordinance who oversaw the manufacture of war machinery and weapons and armour of all kinds. He was responsible for the upkeep of this equipment and had to keep proper records of this material.

FOUR WINGS OF THE ARMY

The Arthashastra describes the functions of the four wings of the army and how they can be deployed to best effect in battle.

CHARIOTS

The chariots had multiple purposes—from acting as a line of defence for the other wings, fending off the enemy's attacks, disrupting the enemy's battle formations and helping one's own scattered ranks to regroup. They also served the purpose of frightening the enemy soldiers, unnerving them with threatening sounds and overwhelming them with a display of magnificence.

ELEPHANTS

Elephants played a crucial role in warfare in ancient India, as mentioned earlier. Their enormous size made them dangerous to opponents—they could bulldoze through battle formations, crush the enemy's foot soldiers, destroy camps and were extremely valuable in sieges. A row of elephants marching in the vanguard of an army could strike terror in the enemy forces. They had other uses, like clearing territory to construct roads, fording rivers, climbing mountains and breaking into inaccessible places. Elephants could also guard the flanks of an army, set fires or extinguish them, demolish ramparts, gates and towers. They could even help transport the loot after a victory. But there was a note of caution too—elephants were not to be employed during the hot, dry season because they needed a lot of water. As for the king who did not own enough elephants, he could make use of donkeys and camels.

HORSES

Horses were useful for scouting battlegrounds, camping sites and forests. They could even locate water sources and, like elephants, ford rivers and devastate the enemy's supplies. Their speed made them efficient in carrying out raids in battle,

breaking enemy formations, chasing the enemy, capturing prisoners, protecting the flanks of the army, keeping soldiers in line and providing support. They could also transport material and captured treasure.

SOLDIERS

The soldiers of the infantry played a variety of roles. They were versatile in the sense that they could fight in all types of terrain. However, they had different kinds of training. Some were more adept at fighting in deserts, others in forests or in marshy areas. Some were skilled in fighting on open land while others were good at trench warfare. Then some could fight better during the day, while others were more effective at night.

When a king set out on a campaign, a well-organized base camp was essential for the optimum performance of his forces. Kautilya advised that it should be close to the battle zone at a place distant from the capital city of the conqueror's kingdom. It was to be near a fort so that the army could retreat into it if the need arose, and the wounded could receive treatment. This semi-permanent township was to mirror the plan of the capital with defences like a moat, towers, battlements, parapets and a gate.

The base camp was envisaged as a place of refuge and was to be at some distance from the actual battlefield. Kautilya also provided advice about the march to the battleground. He gave a lot of importance to the food supplies and suggested that advance information about the capacity of the villages that lay on the route to provide fodder for the animals, fuel and water supplies was essential.

DIFFERENT KINDS OF BATTLES

The Arthashastra describes the various kinds of battles the conqueror can engage in, depending on the circumstances. An open battle in which the place and time have been decided in advance, is recommended if the king is confident about his superiority, has been able to create disaffection in the enemy camp, the terrain and season are amenable and if no other obstacles exist.

If not, the attack should be made when the enemy is in a weak and unguarded position. An enemy can even be enticed into abandoning a secure position by putting on a feint such as a retreat by the conqueror's foreign forces and the jungle tribes.

PREPARING FOR BATTLE

A well-prepared and motivated army was more likely to win. Hence, Kautilya gave several instructions about preparing for battle. The king was to fast the night before the battle and sleep next to his weapons and chariot. He was advised to offer an oblation to the fire as laid out in the Atharva Veda and follow it with prayers for victory, also that those who fell in battle should go to heaven.

Before the battle, he was to give a pep talk to his troops saying that he was as much a servant of the state as they were and they would all share the spoils of war. Then he would urge them to attack the enemy with all their might.

The counsellors and the purohit were to motivate the men next, by lauding their fighting skills and extolling the quality of their battle formations. Astrologers were to foretell victory and bards were to sing songs to exhort the soldiers to fight courageously.

Four basic methods of attack were described, which had also been discussed in the Dhanurveda, an ancient text considered an Upaveda. Battle formations were of utmost importance, and Kautilya described them and suggested what type was suitable on which terrain and according to which situation.

The story of brave Abhimanyu who entered the intricate and dangerous *chakravyuh* formation in the Mahabharata is well-known.

It is worth noting that apart from the Greeks and Romans, few countries had developed such sophisticated formations at that time. The first was the stick or *danda* formation in which the wings, flanks and middle arrays went forward in a row. This was most effective on level ground. The second was the snake or *bhoga*, where they moved in a twisting formation, following each other. This was considered best on uneven ground. The *chakravyuh* of the Mahabharata, was considered an advanced version of this formation. The circle or mandala was one in which they moved together with the men facing in all directions. The mandala represented the circle that represented the universe, and this was the formation Bhishma chose on the seventh day of the Mahabharata war. It was a complex one in which the different divisions of the army were placed together. Kautilya also said that when an attack was expected from the front, the *makara* or crocodile formation was recommended. When expected from the back, *sakata* or cart was suggested. From the two flanks, *vajra* or thunderbolt, and when from all sides a *sarvato badra* or a circular one. On a narrow path, the *suchi* or needle formation—single file was to be followed.

Modern warfare might be far more advanced, but battle formations still have importance because they allow an army to mount an effective attack on the enemy while keeping themselves safe. They can be formations of aircraft, warships, tanks or troops on the ground. Box, column, line, coil and herringbone are a few of them, some of which are adapted from ancient methods of warfare. Formations like the 'V' or wedge are also used by the police when facing rioters.

The directions for an attack were also mentioned. The conqueror was not to launch an attack without supporting troops at the back to shore up the vanguard in case the

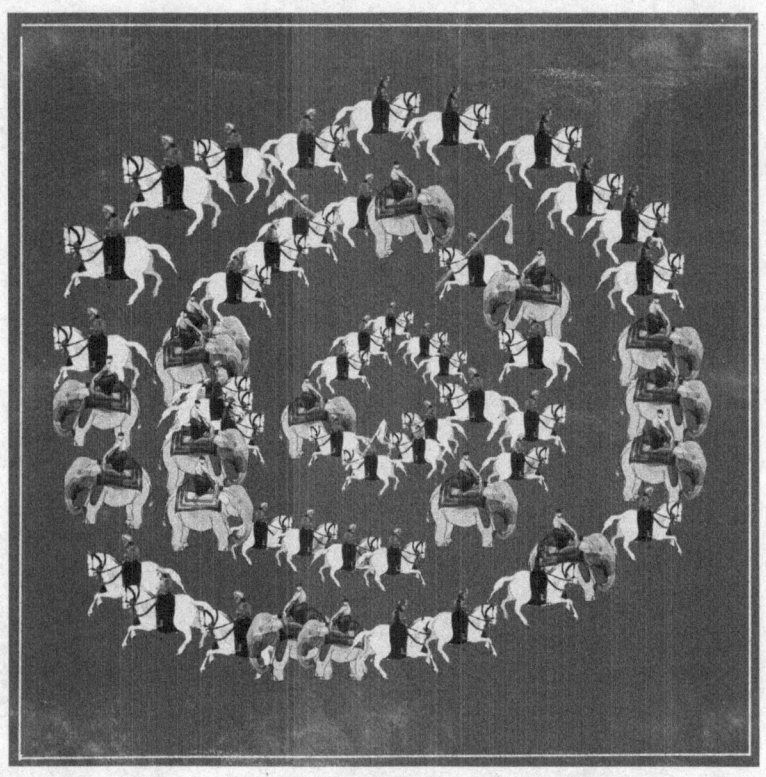

enemy broke through the front positions. As previously mentioned, he was not supposed to lead from the front but accompany the supporting battalions at 360 metres behind the main army.

The enemy was also to be overawed by noise, machinery, occult practices, agents spreading rumours of defeat, false information, proclaiming the invincibility of the conqueror and covertly killing workers. Some of these tactics are still used today in warfare, like in the Russian invasion of Ukraine.

When the enemy retreated into a fort and the king had to lay a siege, various tactics were suggested to lower the morale of the besieged forces, like enticing the starving people to leave the fort, spreading rumours about the invincibility of the king's forces or subverting the enemy commanders. He could also send some of his troops secretly into the fort who would open the gates. This is reminiscent of the Trojan horse episode in the siege of Troy when the Greeks pretended to lift the siege and sail away after hiding their ace warriors in a huge wooden horse. Kautilya also suggested faking a withdrawal and hiding in a forest, then returning to attack when the enemy's guard was down.

Once the battle was won, the conqueror was advised to make peace with a superior foe, negotiate with one equal to him and destroy the weaker. If the vanquished king retreated to his own territory, it was better to let him go. Kautilya was of the opinion that a defeated army was not to be harried further, lest they felt compelled to fight to the death. This shows that he always favoured a balanced approach to avoid excessive bloodshed.

After the conquest of a territory, the victorious king could enjoy the fruits of his labour and relax in the new land, or he could set out on more expeditions. However, the balance of power could have changed in the region and the mandala or circle of kings would have been reset. Former friends might become enemies and with the borders of his kingdom extending, there could be a new natural enemy who was the middle king earlier. The conqueror himself might find himself in the position of the middle or neutral king, or having gained more power, he might find it necessary to eliminate the middle one and then take on the neutral king. If there were no such entities, after establishing himself firmly in the new land, he could deal with the others in the mandala. If the circle of kings did not exist, he could sandwich an enemy between himself and an ally or vice versa. After escalating his power, he could vanquish a weak neighbour who had no allies and having further consolidated his position, move on to a third and fourth one. Once he had established his dominance in the whole region, he could enjoy the position of supreme ruler. However, whatever he did, he was to always follow the principles of dharma.

This is perhaps the knowledge Kautilya put to good use when he helped Chandragupta Maurya establish the first empire in the Indian sub-continent.

What is worth noting, however, is that his military strategy and tactics are still discussed by experts and his methods have been adapted to modern conditions. More so, his theories of governance and foreign policy continue to guide our heads of state. Prime Minister Modi's 'Neighbourhood First' policy to foster economic development in South Asia reflected the sama and dama approach in building friendly relations with Nepal, Bhutan, Bangladesh and Sri Lanka through diplomacy and aid. An understanding of the mandala theory of friendly and unfriendly states is apparent in the strengthening of military alliances with Australia, Japan, Singapore and the USA to counterbalance China's growing power and project India as a vijigishu or leader on the world stage.

Interestingly, during the Cold War, Henry Kissinger, the US Secretary of State who had studied the Arthashastra, built up relations with communist China to isolate the Soviet Union. So, we can see how widespread Kautilya's influence has been.

One thing we need to remember—Kautilya always advocated peace over war and urged the king to put the welfare of his citizens first, over and above his military ambitions. This was amply demonstrated in the breakdown of the Soviet Union which ended the Cold War. With a public dissatisfied with the shortage of consumer goods, an economic downturn and excessive military spending, a time came when their system collapsed. The theory of soft power, using diplomacy and persuasion rather than military supremacy became popular around this time. One of the most enduring images of this era is that of thousands of people queuing up when McDonald's opened its first fast food joint in Moscow in 1990. This amply demonstrated that over two thousand years ago, Kautilya was well aware of what made countries grow and prosper—a satisfied population.

Classic Works on Statecraft

What is the best way to govern a society? How should an ideal state be structured? What traits make a successful ruler? Since the dawn of organized societies, philosophers from various lands and eras have pondered over these questions. Here are a few renowned texts on the art of governance.

Plato's *The Republic*: Born in Athens, Greece, Plato (around 427/428 BCE), a student of Socrates, is among history's most influential thinkers. *The Republic* outlines the blueprint for an ideal state, presented as a dialogue with Socrates. According to Plato, this state comprises three classes: rulers, guardians (soldiers) and producers (farmers and artisans). The philosopher-king, driven by notions of justice and morality, works for the state's well-being. Plato contends that societal harmony hinges on each class fulfilling its role and refraining from overstepping into others' duties.

Aristotle's *Politics*: Another Greek luminary, Aristotle (384–322 BCE), studied under Plato at the Academy in Athens for two decades. As a tutor to Alexander the Great, Aristotle played a pivotal role in shaping the conqueror's pursuits. His brilliance spanned disciplines from logic to zoology, theatre and music. In *Politics*, he extensively examines governance, asserting that a state exists to ensure its citizens' well-being. Active citizen involvement in politics is crucial, he suggests. Aristotle delves into citizenship, laws, constitutions and government forms, ranging from democracy to tyranny. This seminal work continues to inspire political thinkers across generations.

Machiavelli's *The Prince*: Born in Florence, Italy, Niccolò Machiavelli (1469–1527 CE) was a governmental figure and diplomat who experienced turbulent times in Florence's shifting political landscape. After imprisonment and torture, he turned to writing, penning *The Prince*. This work epitomizes realpolitik, advocating rulers to secure power by any means, including manipulation and force. It stresses rulers shouldn't pursue popularity but should instil fear to maintain authority. The term Machiavellian now denotes scheming and unscrupulous behaviour. Although some liken Kautilya to an Indian Machiavelli, the Arthashastra adopts a pragmatic approach without endorsing the ends justifying the means.

Sir Thomas More's *Utopia*: Familiar to us all, 'utopia' signifies an ideal world. Sir Thomas More coined this term, combining Greek words to evoke 'no place' or 'good place'. Written in Latin between 1515–16, *Utopia* envisions an imaginary island marked by order, communal property, gender equality in education, religious tolerance and rational governance. A response to Europe's social and economic inequalities, *Utopia* emerged from More's roles as a lawyer, scholar and public servant. Despite his execution in 1535 for opposing King Henry VIII's break from the Roman Catholic Church, More's influence persists, giving rise to a new English word and a literary genre.

SELECTED BIBLIOGRAPHY

1. Books

Agarwal, Deepa. *Chanakya—The Master of Statecraft*. Gurugram: Puffin, 2013.

Alkazi, Roshen. *Ancient Indian Costume*. New Delhi: National Book Trust India, 1982.

Kangle, R.P. *The Kautilya Arthasastra, (Vol I)*. Mumbai: University of Bombay, 1960.

Kangle, R.P. *The Kautilya Arthasastra, (Vol II)*. New Delhi: Motilal Banarsidass Publishers, 1965.

Kangle, R.P. *The Kautilya Arthasastra, (Vol III)*. New Delhi: Motilal Banarsidass Publishers, 1972.

Mookerji, Radhakumud. *Chandragupta Maurya and His Times*. New Delhi: Motilal Banarsidass Publishers, 1966.

Rangachari, Devika. *The Mauryas*. Noida: Simon and Schuster India, 2022.

Rangarajan, L.N., ed. and trans. *The Arthashastra*. Gurugram: Penguin Random House, 1992.

Shamasastry, R. *Kautilya's Arthashastra*. https://csboa.in/eBooks/Arthashastra_of_Chanakya_-_English.pdf

2. Websites and blogs

Murthy, B.M.N. 'The Scholar Who Discovered Artha Shastra'. Vak Mumbai. Accessed on 16 August 2023, http://www.vakmumbai.org/articles/The%20scholar%20who%20discovered%20artha%20shashtra.pdf

Prakash, Aseem. 'State and Statecraft in Kautilya's Arthashastra.' Indiana University. Accessed on 15 August 2023, https://dlc.dlib.indiana.edu/dlc/bitstream/handle/10535/5647/State%20and%20statecraft%20in%20kautilyas%20arthasastra.pdf

'Women During Chanakya Maurya Era'. Kreately. Accessed on 2 August 2023, https://kreately.in/women-during-chanakya-maurya-era/

'Conceptualizing a Kautilyan Criminal Justice System'. Criminal Law Studies NLUD. Accessed on 11 August 2023, https://criminallawstudiesnluj.wordpress.com/2020/05/10/conceptualizing-a-kautilyan-criminal-justice-system/

Krishnan, B.J. 'The Constitution of India and the Arthashastra'. India Seminar. Available at: https://www.india-seminar.com/2000/492/492%20b.%20j.%20krishnan.htm#:~:text=The%20Constitution%20of%20India%2C%20under,the%20Indian%20Evidence%20Act%201872

Srivastava, Mangalam. 'Essentials of Customary Law in Light of Modern Practice and Judicial Interpretations in

India'. Legal Service India. Available at: https://www. legalserviceindia.com/legal/article-7102-essentials-of-customary-law-in-light-of-modern-practice-and-judicial-interpretations-in-india.html

Afroz. 'Chanakya, His Theory on Geo-politics & its Relevance in Today's World'. Medium. Available at: https://medium.com/@sheikhafroz16/chanakyas-mandal-theory-on-geo-politics-its-relevance-in-today-s-world-e925d07bb351

Gill, Don McLain. 'Kautilya's Silent Wars in Cyberspace'. The Fletcher Forum of World Affairs. Available at: http://www.fletcherforum.org/the-rostrum/2020/7/9/kautilyas-silent-wars-in-cyberspace-1

Gautam, Pradeep Kumar. 'Geopolitics in Chanakya's Arthashastra'. Institute for Defence Studies and Analyses. Available at: https://idsa.in/system/files/jds/10_17-1-2023-Pradeep-Kumar-Gautam.pdf

Singh, Upinder. 'The Puzzle of Ancient Indian Social Structure'. India Seminar. Available at: https://india-seminar.com/2021/738/738_upinder_singh.htm#:~:text=In%20the%20Arthashastra%2C%20as%20in,but%20varna%20is%20the%20foremost

Kamal, Kajari. 'The Relevance of Ancient Indian Strategy in Contemporary Geopolitics'. Observer Research Foundation. Available at: https://www.orfonline.org/research/the-relevance-of-ancient-indian-strategy-in-contemporary-geopolitics/

Dar, Arshid Iqbal. 'Beyond Eurocentrism: Kautilya's realism and India's regional diplomacy'. Nature Communications. Available at: https://www.nature.com/articles/s41599-021-00888-6

Palande, Colonel Deepak. 'Kautilya's Arthashastra and its Relevance in 21st Century'. Centre for Land Warfare Studies. Available at: https://archive.claws.in/images/publication_pdf/1200137411_Kautilya%E2%80%99sArthashastraanditsRelevancein_CLAWS.pdf

Sheikh, Abeed Majid. 'Kautilya, the Indian Machiavelli; On War and Diplomacy in Ancient India' SSRN. Available at: https://papers.ssrn.com/sol3/papers.cfm?abstract_id=3648416

3. Journal

Jindal, Nirmal. 'Relevance of Kautilya in Contemporary International System'. International Journal of Historical Insight and Research (IJHIR), Vol. 5, No. 2, Apr-Jun, 2019.

ACKNOWLEDGMENTS

There are many people who have contributed to this book in different ways, and I am incredibly grateful to all of them. First, I would like to express my gratitude to Sohini Mitra who enthusiastically accepted my proposal for the Arthashastra. As someone very astutely noted, the right editors can profoundly impact a book, and I consider myself fortunate to have had them. Simran Kaur, I extend my heartfelt gratitude to you for fearlessly tackling the unwieldy manuscript that landed on your desk. Your invaluable suggestions have played a monumental role in transforming it into a readable book. Many, many thanks to my copy editor, Prerna Chatterjee—your keen insights and impeccable language instincts have elevated the book to an entirely new level. I thoroughly enjoyed working with both of you.

Many thanks to Gina Mary James for the vibrant cover and design that have greatly enhanced the book's appeal for children and artfully highlighted important elements. Radhika Dinesh, I am truly appreciative of the vivid and striking illustrations that infuse life into the pages. Much gratitude extends to the entire Penguin Random House team, all of whom have contributed to this project.

My heartfelt appreciation goes to esteemed authorities Dr Bibek Debroy and Dr Devika Rangachari, who graciously shared their insights on my work through their quotations.

My husband, Dilip, has consistently provided unwavering support for all my literary ventures, and I am thankful and blessed for his presence. My daughters—Garima, Sonali, and Geetika—have been my pillars of strength, offering unwavering affection, words of encouragement and invaluable guidance on technical matters. What would I do without them? Not to be forgotten are my grandchildren, whose curiosity and fascination with my work continue to be a driving force. Special mention must be made of the youngest, Ahan, who playfully prodded me with constant inquiries about the book's completion and responded with incredulous gasps upon learning it was still a work in progress! This book, indeed, took quite a journey.

My gratitude is extended to the authors of the books I consulted, as well as to those behind the numerous articles and online resources that aided my research. A comprehensive list of these sources can be found in the bibliography.

THE CONSTITUION OF INDIA FOR CHILDREN

Subhadra Sen Gupta

Every 26 January, people gather on New Delhi's Rajpath amidst a colourful jamboree of fluttering flags, marching soldiers and dancing children. What is celebrated on this day is at the heart of our democracy—the magnificent Constitution of India.

The document, which took two years, eleven months and seventeen days to realize, didn't only lay down the law but united India with a vision for the newly independent country. Subhadra Sen Gupta captures the many momentous occasions in Indian history that led to its making in *The Constitution of India for Children*. Populated with facts and dotted with cheerful illustrations, this book provides answers to innumerable questions asked over the years.

Which language is our Constitution written in?
Were women a part of the team that drafted the Constitution?
Why do political parties have symbols next to their names?
What is the official language of India?

An essential handbook for every student and denizen of India, here is a compendium of knowledge that serves as an insightful introduction to the most important document of independent India.

Read More in Puffin

A COMPLETE HISTORY OF INDIA

Roshen Dalal

This book traces the captivating story of Indian history, from the earliest times to the present. It covers all key historical milestones—the advent of the first people, the rise and fall of the Harappan civilization, the emergence of Buddhism and Jainism, prominent dynasties of ancient and medieval India, the arrival of the Europeans, the British regime, the Indian resistance from the Revolt of 1857 to independence, and the nation's progress as a thriving democracy, from 1947 till the present day. It also illuminates Mahatma Gandhi's contribution to the freedom struggle, India during WWII, Partition and its aftermath, the drafting of the Constitution and the enterprise of nation building, and all governments from Jawaharlal Nehru to Narendra Modi.

Going beyond a mere chronological retelling, this well-researched book provides fascinating anecdotes and trivia along with rich illustrations and maps, to make history engaging for young learners.